Games for All Seasons
designed for use in therapeutic riding lessons

Nancy Hohmann

illustrated by
Andrew Ellis

Roadapple Press
2012

Games for All Seasons

Nancy Hohmann

Roadapple Press
420 Crockett Ridge Rd.
Norway, ME 04268

The author and publisher shall not be liable in the event of incident or consequential damages in connection with, or arising out of the instructions and suggestions contained in this book. Neither does the author or publisher have any control over nor assume any responsibility for websites mentioned or their content.

ISBN 978-0615719108

Table of Contents

This book is dedicated to

Julia, who asked every week, "What's today's theme?"

Josh, who asked every week, "What game?"

Nate, who asked about everything!

These three riders were most influential in helping me go beyond "red light, green light"!

Why Games?

Games are an important part of many therapeutic riding lessons. They make the lesson more fun for the riders, volunteers, and the instructor. They grab attention. They keep everyone interested, thinking, and involved. The volunteers enjoy the games as much as the riders do, sometimes even getting into friendly competition with each other. Surprise and variety keep everyone wondering what is coming next.

All these games reinforce basic riding skills: whoa, steering, control at the walk, keeping the proper distance from other horses, trotting and backing up. Students can be on or off lead, but all of them are working on their riding skills while playing the game.

Most of these games can be modified for varying abilities. Some riders get lots of information about the theme of the day; others just play a simplified version. More-challenged riders get help from volunteers.

Riders learn social skills: to take turns, to encourage one another, and to work as a team with volunteers. Riders learn to speak up, focus, problem solve (How do you carry a mud boot while holding the reins?), follow directions, communicate.

Games help riders increase balance. Riders have to lean over, reach, carry things, use a hand for swatting, flipping, tossing. Games can reinforce a rider's personal goals: to ride without holding the trot strap, to whoa independently, to follow two-step directions. Games heighten a rider's imagination and sense of fair play. Riders learn about appropriate competition.

Not every game is competitive or a race. When games appear to be competitive, the focus is on the good things that each rider does while playing. Riders cheer each other on. Some horses are just too slow to actually win any kind of "race". Everyone wins in some way, be it by form or by time, or by attitude.

Some riders think they can't do a particular game. I've never found that to be the case. One rider often says, "Too hard!" but the last time he said that, he won the game.

Games encourage speaking and social interaction. Many games require an answer to a question. Usually ANY answer gets positive reinforcement; in other words, if you don't know, make something up! Sometimes the riders come up with some very funny answers and spark interesting discussion.

How to Build Your Own Game

After you're tired of the games in this book, create your own. First choose a theme, perhaps using the calendar, current events, things that have to do with horses, things that interest you, things that have to do with your state, things that have to do with one of the riders (trips, interests, etc.), famous people, popular books for kids, common items (the pencil, the potato, the turkey). Many tie into the greater community, history, local events. Interestingly, I have found that if I do repeat a game, the kids have remembered much more about the theme than I thought they would.

Next, do some research on your theme. I use the internet mostly. For the Superbowl, for instance, I knew almost nothing about football, but had enough information in fifteen minutes using the internet to create a game. You don't need piles of information, just a few interesting facts.

Then gather your props -- from the basement, a discount store, yard sales, your kids' toy box. Make sure the props will not upset a horse and will not endanger a rider. Think soft and bendable. Use your imagination to figure out an activity that ties to the props, and present the activity with confidence and enthusiasm. Pool noodles and Kwiktwists (www.kwiktwist.com , also available at Tractor Supply Company and Lowes) are very helpful. Straws, pipe cleaners, flat foam sheets, a white board, and plastic flamingos all have their place in the arena along with those dressage letters! If you laminate your photos and drawings, you'll have them for next year.

Games are great fun, but there is a time and a place for everything. Sometimes there is no room for playing games. Sometimes the horse has his own work to do, and it is your job to get out of the way and let him work his magic. So as much as I recommend games, know their place and use them appropriately.

How This Book Is Arranged

The games in this book are presented based on the calendar and are arranged by month. Some games are not particularly tied to the calendar and can be played any time, even though they are listed under a certain month. After December's games there is a section on various other ideas. There are enough games to get you through a year of lessons and then some. Each game includes ideas for stretches. Please note that all ideas for stretches are for **pantomiming**. Every game includes detailed information about equipment needed and arena set up. Have fun!

N.B. A white board mounted in the arena is very handy for many of these games. You can substitute a piece of poster paper, foam core, or chalk board.

Standard dressage lettering is used throughout to describe placement in the arena.

Games for January

Happy New Year Around the World
Happy Birthday, Martin Luther King, Jr.
Inauguration Day Parade
Snowflakes
Let's Build a Snowman
Let's Go Skijoring!

Happy New Year Around the World

This is a game involving riding over poles and finding things in the arena. Riders will learn customs concerning New Year celebrations from Greece, Japan, Brazil, and the Netherlands.

Equipment needed
•seven ground poles
•lots of small stuffed toys
•a bucket per rider
•laminated photos of flames or a bonfire (one per rider)
•laminated photos of presents, or small boxes (one per rider)
•laminated photos of lobsters (one per rider)
•a fake Christmas tree mounted on a pole (You'll need one or two for Christmas anyway.)

Set up
•Place seven ground poles parallel to each other up the center of the arena.
•Place stuffed toys around the arena on railings, in reach.
•Place a bucket per rider at one end of arena.
•Place the Christmas tree in the arena, probably toward the center.
•Place all photos around the arena.

•Skills
•riding: riding over ground poles, two-point if appropriate, steering, whoa, standing still, walk on
•gross and fine motor skills
•balance
•following directions

Introduction to the game
During meet and greet, ask the riders how they celebrate New Year's Day. Tell them today they will celebrate the way people in several countries do. In Brazil people jump seven waves for good luck. We will "jump" (walk) over seven "waves" (poles). In Japan people clean the house, laugh, and have lobster. We will clean the arena, laugh, and find lobster. In Greece people exchange presents. We'll look for presents and pass them. In the Netherlands people pile up the used Christmas trees and have bonfires. We'll put the flames on the Christmas tree.

During stretches riders can wave seven times, "sweep," laugh, pretend to eat lobster, and pretend to open presents.

At game time
If you have not already used the poles throughout the lesson, now is the time. Pretend to jump the waves and say, "Happy New Year." Ride in two-point where appropriate. For the Japanese clean up, start each rider at one of the buckets. Give them a certain amount of time, perhaps three minutes, to collect as many toys as possible and put them into the buckets. There needs to be a lot of laughing to chase off the bad luck. Each rider should also find a lobster at this time. The lobster, due to its curved back, represents old age and gives one the hope of living to an old age. At the end of the allotted time, count to see who gathered up the most toys.

Now search for and retrieve the presents. Have each rider offer a present to someone in the arena.

Next, find the flames; put them on the Christmas tree; and say "Happy New Year" in many languages!

French: bonne année
Spanish: feliz año nuevo
Hawaiian: hauoli makahiki hou
Chinese: gun hay fat choy

. . . .

Happy Birthday, Martin Luther King, Jr.
This game introduces the concept of equality for all while celebrating a birthday.

Equipment needed
•picture of a birthday cake
•dove, (photo, drawing, or stuffed animal)
•numbers 3 and 9
•optional: bookmarks with the "I Have a Dream" quote (available at www.ActivityVillage.co.uk)

Set up
•"Hide" the dove, birthday cake, and numbers 3 and 9 around the arena.

Skills
•riding: walk on, whoa, steering, standing still
•listening
•speaking/singing

Introduction to the game
During meet and greet, ask riders why they have a day off from school this week, or last week. Ask if anyone has heard of MLK, Jr and why he is important. Read the first part of his speech: "I have a dream that my four little children will one day live in a nation where they will not be judged by the color of their skin but by the content of their character." Discuss as riders are able to understand. Today there will be a birthday celebration for Martin Luther King, Jr.

During stretches have riders make the peace sign, stretching way above heads. They can do all stretches while holding the peace sign if they wish. Blow out the birthday candles.

At game time
Riders come to the center of the arena or to the white board, or poster board. Send riders out to find the dove of peace, the birthday cake, and the numbers 3 and 9, explaining that MLK, Jr lived only until age 39. When all is found, bring it back to the white board, poster board, or instructor, and assemble the cake and numbers with dove nearby. Sing happy birthday to Martin and say thank you to him for working for equal rights for all.

Inauguration Day Parade (January 20, every four years)

Although this game comes only once every four years, it is really worth celebrating with a parade. This is more fun if there are a few riders.

Equipment needed
•a small American flag for each rider -- You can use a photo taped to a straw.
•a photo of the White House
•a photo of the Capitol
•a recording of "Hail to the Chief"

Set up
•Place a large photo of the Capitol at C.
•Place a large photo of the White House at A.
•Have small flags nearby.

Skills
•riding: walk on, matching speed of horse to others in arena, keeping proper distance from other horses, steering
•fine motor skills
•sensory integration

Introduction to the game
During meet and greet, ask riders what is important about January 20th this year. Discuss who the president is, who the new one is, and what a president does, as riders are capable of understanding. During stretches there should be a lot of waving and shaking hands! Today there will be a parade to welcome the new president to the White House.

At game time
Hand each rider a flag and explain proper use of same, and how to hold and wave it safely while holding the reins in the other hand. Play "Hail to the Chief" and parade from the Capitol to the White House, keeping horses together and waving to "the crowd."

• • • • • • • • • • • • • •

Snowflakes

This is a game that combines riding a pattern with learning about snowflakes.

Equipment needed
•large laminated numbers, 1 through 6
•six different photographs, or drawings, or cutouts of snowflakes -- Ideally these will be copies of photographs by Wilson "Snowflake" Bentley. Refer to www.snowflakebentley.com.
•optional: copy of the children's book Snowflake Bentley by Jacqueline Briggs Martin

Set up
•Place the number 1 and a snowflake photo at C.
•Place the number 2 and a snowflake photo at A.
•Place the number 3 and a snowflake at M.

•Place the number 4 and a snowflake at K.
•Place the number 5 and a snowflake at H.
•Place the number 6 and a snowflake at F.
•Place a cone, post, or hula hoop at X.

Skills
•riding: steering, whoa, keeping proper distance from other horses
•listening
•following directions
•sequencing

Introduction to the game
At meet and greet, tell the riders the theme for the day is snowflakes and ask what they know about them. Snow is the simplest form of frozen precipitation. For it to snow, temperatures must be at or below freezing at all levels of the atmosphere. The snowiest city in the US is Blue Canyon, CA, with 240" of annual snowfall. The 5th snowiest city in the US is Caribou, ME, with 110" of annual snowfall. Yes, there is snow in Hawaii, in the mountains over 5,000'. No two snowflakes are alike.

During stretches, riders make snow fall with their fingers. They shovel snow, throw snowballs, and eat snow cones. They hug themselves to keep warm in the snow.

At game time
Meet the Instructor at X. Wilson "Snowflake" Bentley was the first person to photograph a snowflake in 1885, showing us that all snowflakes have six sides. He lived in Jericho, VT, and took over 5,000 pictures. He caught snowflakes on a blackboard and transferred them to a microscope slide. He had a compound microscope attached to a bellows camera. Riders will ride the following pattern, starting off one at a time and paying attention to other riders at all times: 1 to X to 2 to X to 3 to X to 4 to X to 5 to X to 6 to X. Notice the snowflakes at the numbers. At the end you will have ridden a snowflake.

....

Let's Build a Snowman!
In this game, riders will decorate a "snowman" with everything they need to make him, or her, look "real."

Equipment needed
•a large drawing of the outline of a snowman on poster paper, or foam core board, preferably laminated
•eyes, nose, mouth, top hat, scarf, buttons for the snowman -- These can be the actual items (scarf, top hat, carrot, buttons, chunks of coal) or made of cardboard or poster paper with tape on the backs.
•something to hang the snowman on, such as a whiteboard, easel or wall of arena
•or, a drawing of a snowman on a whiteboard

Set up
•Hang the blank snowman in the arena.
•Place the snowman accessories around the arena for the riders to find.

Skills
•riding: steering, whoa, riding with something in hand
•large motor skills
•coordination
•cooperation

Introduction to game
Everybody knows how to build a snowman. At meet and greet, ask who has ever built a snowman, how tall, what accessories, how long did it last, etc. During stretches roll up the snowballs and pile them up. Pat the snowman and mime decorating him.

At game time
Riders gather at the blank snowman and set off to find the parts, returning with one part at a time to decorate the snowman. Maybe he or she needs a name, too.

. . . .

Let's Go Skijoring!
This is an obstacle course with a twist.

Equipment needed
•several laminated photos of people skijoring -- Google "skijoring behind a horse" and enough images to take your breath away will pop up.
•a laminated drawing of a person on skis, with a helmet and goggles on, holding reins -- He will "ride" behind the rider on the horse's rump. My person is about ten inches tall. If you have a stuffed figure of a skier, that could also work. Give him or her a name!
•one ground pole or cavaletti
•several cones on posts
•several plastic rings -- The kind you dive for in a swimming pool work well.
•optional: stopwatch to time riders

Set up
•Set up a simple obstacle course in the arena including a cavaletti, a cone on a post with a ring to be picked up, some cones on posts to weave in and out of, similar to pole bending. The last cone on a post is to be placed at the end of the course. This will be where the rider places the ring he picked up earlier, finishing the course.
•Place photos of people skijoring around the arena.
•Have your "skijoring person" handy.

Skills
•riding: riding over ground poles, steering, whoa, trotting if appropriate
•gross/fine motor skills
•following directions
•memory

•competition
•taking turns

Introduction to the game
At meet and greet, ask if anyone has heard of skijoring. Skijoring began behind reindeer in Scandinavia as a way to travel. In the 1928 Olympics there was a demonstration of skijoring with a horse, but there was no rider on the horse. In 1949 the "modern" game of skijoring with a rider and someone on skis behind began in Leadville, CO. The event is timed, has jumps, gates, rings to be speared, and twists and turns, all at a gallop!

During stretches, work for "strength training," as skijoring takes incredible strength. Make muscles, do push ups, sit ups, twist at the waist, reach for rings, touch toes, knees, and anything else to make you strong.

At game time
Assemble at the start of the obstacle course. Put the skijoring "person" on the rump of the horse who is going through the course, or tape it to the saddle pad behind the saddle. Remind the rider that he must NOT lose his skijoring friend! Explain the course, or walk through it. Time it or not. Walking or trotting. Cheer everyone on through the course, one at a time!

Games for February

Groundhog Day, February 2
Super Bowl
Valentine's Day
Winter Olympic Games: curling, pair skating, biathlon
Chinese New Year
Mardi Gras
Presidents' Day Treasure Hunt
Happy Birthday, Henry Wadsworth Longfellow

Groundhog Day, February 2

This is a game about the groundhog tradition, with riders having the option to decide the future weather. Riders also learn other interesting facts about February 2nd.

Equipment needed
•large photo of a real groundhog, laminated
•large drawings or photos of a groundhog coming out of a hole and looking around, one per rider
•cutouts of clouds, one per rider, laminated
•cutouts of suns, laminated, one per rider
•optional: Put a hole in the bottom of a plastic cup with a pencil. Cut out a drawing or photo small enough to fit inside the cup of a ground hog sitting up. Tape it on the end of the pencil. Pass the pencil down through the cup. Pull the groundhog down into the cup, then have him peek up and look around. You can even sing this song to the tune of "I'm a Little Teapot":
I' m a little groundhog furry and brown.
I'm coming up to look around.
If I see my shadow down I'll go.
Then six more weeks of winter, oh no!
•optional: pictures of Punxsutawney Phil

Set up
•Place one drawing/photo of a groundhog per rider on the far side of the arena.
•On the opposite side of the arena place one sun and one cloud per rider.
•Have a photo of a real groundhog somewhere in the arena for riders to see.

Skills
•riding: steering, reverse turn, walk on
•decision making
•listening
•speaking
•gross motor skills

Introduction to the game
At meet and greet, ask who knows what February 2nd is. Groundhog Day goes back to a pagan holiday. Europeans originally used a hedgehog to predict whether there would be an early spring or a long winter. Since there were no hedgehogs in the US, a groundhog was chosen. Show photos of Punxsutawney Phil if possible.

February 2 is also Candlemas Day, or the purification of Mary, during which there were candle processions. Six weeks after Christmas, Mary and candles were blessed at the temple.

It is half way to spring, and a "looking ahead" holiday. Discuss the proverb: "Half your wood and half your hay you should still have on Candlemas Day." This is a good day to focus on looking where you are going! Look where you are going or you will go where you're looking. During stretches be sure to look where you are going. Next, put your hand to your forehead and look around. Shrug your shoulders. Make a sun with your arms. Make clouds with your arms. Be a groundhog scurrying back to his burrow. Be a groundhog eating grass.

At game time

Meet riders at the end of the arena where the suns and clouds are placed. Explain that if the groundhog sees his shadow from the sun shining he will be scared and run into his burrow. We will have a longer winter. If it is cloudy, he will stay up longer and nibble some grass. Spring will come early.

Riders are to choose a sun or a cloud, ride to the groundhog, place the sun or cloud near the groundhog and ride back. When they arrive back they need to tell the group what they placed near the groundhog and what it means.

. . . .

Super Bowl (the first Sunday in February)

Riders will carry a football the length of the arena, moving ahead by answering questions about football.

Equipment needed
•one real or toy football
•one coin to flip
•one "goal post" made with Kwiktwists on a post
•one set of question cards with answers on back, as follows:

> --What is this number? (write current Superbowl number in Roman numerals)
> --How much does a 30-second advertisement cost? (Check the internet; in 2011 it cost $2.8 million.)
> --When did football start in the US? 1840's
> --How many players are on the field per team? eleven
> --How long is the field between goal posts? 100 yards
> --How many tries does the offensive team have to move the ball ten yards? four
> --How many minutes in a quarter? fifteen in professional ball, usually twelve in high school
> --How many minutes of play in a professional game? 60
> --What teams are playing this year? (obviously varies each year)
> --Who is performing at half time this year? (check the internet)
> --How long is the pre-show? (in 2011 it was four hours!)
> --Who receives the snap from the center on most plays? Quarter Back

Set up
•Place goal post at the far end of the arena.
•Have the question cards and coin handy.

Skills
•riding: walk on, whoa, counting horse foot steps, standing still
•speaking
•following directions
•teamwork
•competition

Introduction to the game
During meet and greet, ask who is going to watch the Superbowl. During stretches, practice "throwing" a football, catching, running to the goalpost, raising hands in touchdown symbol, carrying football.

At game time
Riders assemble side by side at the end of the arena opposite the goal post. With the flip of a coin, determine who will carry the football. That person is asked the first question. Ask questions to one rider at a time. The rider may consult volunteers. If the rider doesn't know the answer, he/she should make a guess. If the rider carrying the football gets the answer wrong, he/she must pass the football to the next rider. If the answer is correct, move ahead 3 steps. If wrong, but made a guess, move ahead 2 steps. (You can adjust the steps according to your time limit and size of arena.) Continue asking questions.

When a rider gets close to the goal post, he/she may attempt a goal by throwing the ball through the posts. If he/she doesn't have the ball, he/she may try to answer another question to get the ball back. All riders may have a chance to throw for a goal.

. . . .

Valentine's Day (February 14)
Riders celebrate the holiday by making Valentines for their horses and learning about the origin of the tradition.

Equipment needed
•one small clipboard with marker attached per rider
•at least one paper heart per rider, on clipboard
•various stickers for decorating the Valentines
•mailbox for Valentine cards
•optional: Make "Valentine wands" by taking a red or pink pipe cleaner, shaping it into a heart and placing the pointed ends of the heart into a drinking straw.

Set up
•Place clipboards with markers, stickers, and paper hearts in the arena.
•Place Valentine wands in the arena.
•Place mailbox in the arena where riders can reach and open it (on a barrel, or attached to a rail, for instance).

Skills
•riding: walk on, whoa, standing still
•writing
•fine motor skills
•communication
•creativity

Introduction to game

At meet and greet, ask riders what they know about Valentine's Day, how it got its name, and how we celebrate it. Valentine's Day was first celebrated in the US in 1931. Saint Valentine was a real priest who was killed in Rome on February 14 in the year 269. Claudius II, Emperor of Rome and also known as Claudius the Cruel, had declared there could be no marriages because he wanted all the men for his army. Valentine was secretly marrying couples against the Emperor's will. He was caught and sent to jail, where legend has it he fell in love with the jailer's daughter who befriended him. On the day he was executed, he sent her a thank you letter for her kindness and signed it, "Love from your Valentine."

During stretches today, make the shape of a heart with your fingers in the air. Start making it small, then make it bigger and bigger. How big can you make it?

At game time

Hand each rider a clipboard and ask him or her to make a Valentine for his or her horse. Volunteers may help! Afterwards ride to the mailbox and place the Valentines inside. Riders may make more Valentines if time allows. Pick up a Valentine wand and say something kind to every person in the arena as you wave the wand in that person's direction.

. . . .

Winter Olympic Games: curling, pair skating, biathlon

It doesn't have to be an Olympic year since athletes are always in training. Winter Olympics take place in February. These are highly modified versions of the above games.

Equipment needed

• two portable, free standing basketball hoops -- These can be made with a swim noodle made into a circle with duct tape and placed on a post with a Kwiktwist, or use a plastic toy basketball hoop.
• large, soft balls to be used as basketballs
• a hula hoop
• two bean bags per rider, same color per rider, but different colors per team
• skating music and a way to play it
• optional: stop watch for biathlon

Set up

•Place the hula hoop on the ground in the center of the arena.
•Have bean bags handy.
•Place one basketball hoop at one end of the arena, and the second at the opposite end.

Skills

•riding: walk on, whoa, standing still, steering, riding side by side, keeping proper distance from other horses, trotting if appropriate
•gross motor skills
•following directions
•competition

•sensory integration
•counting

Introduction to the game

At meet and greet, ask riders if they can name any winter Olympic sports. Tell them they will participate in three today: curling, biathlon, and pair skating. During stretches riders should reach as high as possible, practice shooting a basketball, practice "sliding" a stone for curling, and do other stretches for strength training. What exercises would an Olympian do?

Curling began in the 1500's in Scotland. It became an Olympic sport in 1998, and was introduced in the US in the 1830's when the Scots brought it to Michigan. Four people make up a team. The target for the 42 pound granite rock is called the house, is twelve feet in diameter, and is forty-two yards away. Sweepers travel up to two miles in a game trying to make the stone travel farther and straighter. The stone is released with a slow, underhand motion.

Biathlon combines cross country skiing and rifle shooting. It began in Norway as a type of military training. Competitors ski, then shoot at 5 targets, continue skiing and shoot again. There are usually two or four shooting rounds. Scoring is by time and shooting accuracy.

Pair skating has been part of the Olympics since 1924. Ice skating was originally developed as a means of transportation.

At game time

Begin with curling. Riders meet instructor at one end of the arena with a hula hoop placed an appropriate distance away depending on capabilities of riders. (twelve feet?) Each rider gets two bean bags which are tossed underhand toward the hula hoop. After all bean bags have been tossed, those closest to the center of the hoop score more. Invent your own scoring so everyone wins or gets second chances.

For the biathlon, riders ride along the rail at a walk or trot to the first basketball hoop. Each rider take five shots, keeping track of how many go in. Riders walk or trot to the next basketball hoop. Each rider takes five shots again, adding to the score for every ball in. Ride to end of the course as determined by the instructor. Use time and number of hoops to determine the winner if you want to have a winner.

For pair skating, riders ride side by side to skating music, circling, crossing the diagonal, whatever comes to mind. Riders work on keeping horses together, but an appropriate distance from each other.

· · · · · · · · · · · · · ·

Chinese New Year

The date varies from the end of January to mid February. Check the internet for the date for a particular year. This game is a take off of egg and spoon and acts out some Chinese traditions.

Equipment needed

•one large spoon for each rider
•one bucket per rider

•one red envelope per rider with pretend money inside and the words "gung hey fat choy"
•an orange or tangerine per rider
•optional: paper lanterns for "lantern parade"
•optional: Chinese music

Set up
•Place a spoon and an orange or tangerine in a bucket, one per rider, at one end of the arena.
•Place a cone or post opposite the bucket at the other end of the arena.
•"Hide" one red envelope per rider around the arena.
•Have paper lanterns handy in arena, if you are doing a lantern parade.

Skills
•riding: walk on, whoa, steering, reverse turn, steering with reins in one hand
•focus
•problem solving
•balance

Introduction to game
At meet and greet, ask if anyone has heard of the Chinese New Year. It is also called the Spring Festival and is the longest and most important holiday in China. It begins on a different day each year, based on a lunisolar calendar: the eve of the first day of the first month in the lunisolar calendar, the second new moon after the winter solstice. It ends the fifteenth day with a lantern festival. Each year has a different animal associated with it, which can add to your presentation.

There are many customs associated with this holiday, and they vary. Here are a few: Clean the house, sweep away bad luck, let happiness, wealth, and longevity in. Open the windows at midnight. Wear red clothing for good luck, and decorate with red. Red scares away evil spirits and the sound of the word for red (hong) means prosperous. Go see your family. Forget grudges, and wish for peace and happiness. Children get red envelopes with money on the first day of the festival.

How is Chinese New Year's alike or different from any of our holidays? During stretches, sweep the house clean, open the windows, offer a smile and wave to everyone, shoo the evil spirits away.

At game time
Meet at the buckets. Face the cones or posts at the opposite end of the arena. Tangerines and oranges represent good health and long life. Give each rider a spoon and a piece of fruit. The rider must carry the fruit in the spoon to the post, circle it (All go to the right around the post.) and come back to the bucket. Rider places the spoon in the bucket and may keep the fruit for good health.

Next send riders off to find red envelopes which are "hidden" in the arena. Inside the envelope it says, "gung hey fat choy" which means "wishing you prosperity and wealth." All try to say that to each other. You may then put on some Chinese music, pick up the paper lanterns and have a lantern parade.

Mardi Gras

This holiday changes each year also. It is the day before Ash Wednesday. This game is a variation of egg and spoon: pancake on spatula. Riders learn the true meaning of Mardi Gras.

Equipment needed
•one plastic spatula per rider
•one bucket per rider
•one real pancake per rider, with extras "in case"
•one mask per rider and volunteer

You can use any variety of masks, but for safety I made small eye masks out of foam sheets and taped each one to a drinking straw. The riders and volunteers carry the masks in front of their eyes. Nothing is strapped on, it's easy to see, but all are "hiding" behind the masks. You can add feathers and sequins if you care to get fancy, or leave them plain.
•optional: beads for riders and volunteers
•optional: parade music

Set up
•Place buckets with pancakes and spatulas at one end of the arena.
•Place a post or a cone opposite each bucket at the far end of the arena.
•Have masks and beads handy.

Skills
•riding: riding with one hand at the walk including steering and whoa
•focus
•balance
•following directions
•sensory integration

Introduction to the game
At meet and greet, ask if anyone knows what "Mardi Gras" means. It is French for Fat Tuesday, and comes the day before Ash Wednesday. Ash Wednesday is the first day of the six-week period called Lent which precedes Easter. Because it was once traditional for many people to forego fattening foods during Lent, Mardi Gras became the day to use up the butter, eggs, and sugar. In France that meant making pancakes, and pancake contests and races were popular. Mardi Gras in New Orleans is a big party before the more serious time of Lent, and is celebrated with parades, parties, and masked balls.

During stretches today, beat up some pancake batter, flip the pancakes, eat them. From your parade horse throw candy to the people watching. Wave to everyone at the parade. Pretend to dance at the ball.

At game time
Have riders meet at the buckets. Hand each rider a spatula with a pancake on it. Riders proceed to the post at the other end of the arena, circle it (all keeping to the right of the post), and return to the bucket. Flip the pancake into the bucket and hand the volunteer or instructor the spatula. Many horses love pancakes, so depending on the rules of your barn, offer the horses a pancake treat.
Pass out masks and beads to all riders and volunteers and parade once around the arena, waving to the crowds. Put on the parade music if you have some.

....

Presidents' Day Treasure Hunt

Presidents' Day is the third Monday of February. This game takes some preparation and set up, but all the information is provided below. It is a traditional treasure hunt using facts about George Washington, Abraham Lincoln, and Teddy Roosevelt. Up to three riders can play at the same time, but it can be easily modified for one, two, or even more than three if riders work in pairs.

Equipment needed
For this game I used pictures printed from the internet. You will need to select and print your own. I put each picture in a plastic sleeve protector (fits standard printer paper). It is a bit time consuming to prepare, but is a lot of fun for all and can be used again easily.

•pictures of George Washington, Abraham Lincoln, and Teddy Roosevelt.
•four clues for each president, each with a picture on front, and directions for the next clue on the back.

Below is the list of pictures, with the information for the back of each picture written beneath it.

George Washington
I am George Washington, the first President of the United States. For my inauguration I rode in a yellow and black carriage pulled by four white horses. Ride to the picture of the four white horses.

Four white horses
How do you usually clean a horse? We were "painted" with a paste of ground chalk and water the day before the inauguration and wrapped in linen. The next day we were brushed, even our teeth! Ride to the picture of horse teeth.

Horse teeth
George Washington had his groom brush his horses' teeth every day. He certainly knew the importance of teeth! He also bred and raised mules. Ride to the picture of a mule.

Mule
A mule is a cross of a horse and a donkey. One of George Washington's favorite horses was called Blueskin. He was a gray horse. Ride to the picture of George Washington with a gray horse.

Painting of George Washing standing with gray horse
I am Blueskin, but another favorite horse of George Washington was named Nelson, and he was a bay.
Trot back to the center of the arena and whoa. Make sure you can share one fact you learned about George Washington.

Abraham Lincoln
I am Abraham Lincoln, the sixteenth President of the United States. I grew up with horses. As a young boy, I worked at a grist mill making the horses go round and round to grind the grain. Ride to the picture of a millstone.

Millstone
This stone is a millstone used to grind grain. As an adult Lincoln owned riding horses and driving horses. One of his driving horses was stolen. Ride to the picture of the horse and carriage.

Horse and carriage
Lincoln rode and read law books at the same time! Ride to the picture of the statue of Lincoln reading while on the back of a horse.

Statue of Lincoln reading while on a horse
When Lincoln was President, he often rode a very tall, thin horse called "Abe" (named after him). It was difficult to find stirrup leathers long enough for the President. Ride to a picture of a stirrup leather.

Stirrup leather
Lincoln's sons Tad and Willie had ponies at the White House. Trot back to the center o the arena and be sure you can share one fact you learned about Abraham Lincoln.

Teddy Roosevelt
I am Teddy Roosevelt, the twenty-sixth President of the United States. As a young man I had a ranch in North Dakota and raised cattle. I learned to ride western. Ride to a picture of a western saddle.

Western saddle
Teddy Roosevelt was a leader of the Rough Riders during the Spanish-American War. Ride to a picture of him on his horse. Notice his large sword!

Theodore Roosevelt in his Rough Riding days, carrying a sword, on horseback
Teddy Roosevelt took his five children on point to point hikes, and they had to go in a straight line right over anything in the way. He also loved to jump horses. Ride straight across the arena to a picture of someone jumping on horseback.

Picture of someone jumping on horseback
Teddy Roosevelt had ten horses and one black and white pony, Algonquin, at the White House. Ride to the picture of Quentin (Teddy's son) on Algonquin.

Picture of Quentin on Algonquin (www.presidentialpetmuseum.com)
Here is Algonquin with Quentin riding. Once Quentin took Algonquin inside the White House and up the elevator to see Archie, Quentin's brother, who was sick. Now trot back to the center of the arena, and be sure you can share one fact you learned about Teddy Roosevelt.

Set up
•Place the first three pictures side by side along one side of the arena.
•Place the other pictures around the arena, making sure riders have to move around to find the next clue.

Skills
•riding: walk on, whoa, standing still, trotting, steering, keeping proper distance from other horses
•reading
•listening
•memory
•communication
•following directions
•focus

Introduction to the game
At meet and greet, ask the riders what they know about Presidents' Day. Tell them they will each have a president to learn about later. Stretches should include pretending to drive a carriage, pretending to read a book while riding, waving, and getting into two- point position.

At game time
Riders gather in the center of the arena facing the pictures of the three presidents. Each rider chooses or is assigned a different president. Riders ride to the first picture and follow the clues. At the end, when all are done, each rider shares one fact about his or her president.

. . . .

Happy Birthday, Henry Wadsworth Longfellow February 27
This lesson is also appropriate for Patriots Day in April, a holiday celebrated in Maine and Massachusetts. Riders read and act out parts of "The Midnight Ride of Paul Revere."

Equipment needed
•a sign reading "the opposite shore"
•separate signs reading Medford, Lexington, and Concord
•picture of the tower of the Old North Church
•pictures of two old-fashioned lanterns -- www.paul-revere-heritage.com/one-if-by-land-two-if-by-sea has pictures of the lantern, the tower, and drawings of Paul on his horse.
•seven cards with quotes from Longfellow and directions, as explained below:

1.
Listen, my children, and you shall hear
Of the midnight ride of Paul Revere,
On the eighteenth of April, in Seventy-five,

Hardly a man is now alive
Who remembers that famous day and year...
He said to his friend, "If the British march
By land or sea from the town tonight,
Hang a lantern aloft in the belfry arch
Of the North Church tower as a signal light,
One if by land, and two, if by sea,
And I on the opposite shore will be,
Ready to ride and spread the alarm
Through every Middlesex village and farm,
For the country folk to be up and to arm.

directions: RIDE TO THE OPPOSITE SHORE.

2.

Meanwhile, impatient to mount and ride,
Booted and spurred, with a heavy stride,
On the opposite shore walked Paul Revere.
Now he patted his horse's side,
Now gazed at the landscape far and near,
Then, impetuous, stamped the earth,
And turned and tightened his saddle-girth.

directions: PAT YOUR HORSE. CHECK THE GIRTH. LOOK AT THE TOWER OF THE OLD NORTH CHURCH.

3.

He springs to the saddle, the bridle he turns,
But lingers and gazes, till full on his sight
A second lamp in the belfry burns!

directions: TROT TO MEDFORD. YELL, "THE BRITISH ARE COMING!"

4.

It was 12 by the village clock
When he crossed the bridge into Medford town.

directions: TROT TO LEXINGTON. YELL, "THE BRITISH ARE COMING!"

5.

It was one by the village clock
When he galloped into Lexington.

directions: TROT TO CONCORD. YELL, "THE BRITISH ARE COMING!"

6.

It was 2 by the village clock
When he came to the bridge in Concord town.

In the hour of darkness and peril and need,
The people will waken and listen to hear
The hurrying hoofbeats of that steed,
And the midnight message of Paul Revere.

directions: TROT TO THE BARREL FOR BLOWING BUBBLES AND CELEBRATING.

7.
Lives of great men all remind us
We can make our lives sublime,
And, departing, leave behind us
Footprints on the sands of time.

Make straight footprints down the center line of the arena.
What do you want to be when you grow up?

Set up
•Place signs around the arena for "the opposite shore" at E, Medford at C, Lexington at B, and Concord at A.
•Place a picture of the tower and two lanterns by it at B.
•Have all poem cards handy. I keep them in my pocket.
•Set up a bubble station on a barrel for celebrating Longfellow's birthday.

Skills
•riding: walk on, trotting, whoa, steering, standing still, riding in a straight line
•listening
•following directions
•speaking
•blowing bubbles

Introduction to the game
At meet and greet, ask if anyone has heard of Henry Wadsworth Longfellow, a very popular poet in the 1800s. He was born in Portland, Maine, went to Bowdoin College at age fourteen, and taught at Harvard University. Some may be familiar with his poem which begins, "Under a spreading chestnut tree/ The village smithy stands". When the chestnut tree Longfellow wrote about was chopped down, a group of children paid to have a chair made from its wood for his 72nd birthday. What is a smithy?

For stretches today applaud, say hooray and throw your arms up in the air, pretend to blow up balloons, and pretend to eat cake.

At game time
Gather riders at A prepared to ride to the "the opposite shore" and read card number one. Follow the directions on the card. Proceed through card six around the arena. Then celebrate by blowing bubbles and singing happy birthday to Henry. To end the lesson, read card seven and have riders follow the directions.

Games for March

Dr. Seuss Day
The Iditarod
Shamrock Races
Ice Fishing
Build an Igloo

Dr. Seuss Day

This game is based on <u>And to Think That I Saw It on Mulberry Street.</u> Essentially it is pole bending with a Dr. Seuss theme.

Equipment needed
•a copy of the book <u>And to Think That I Saw It on Mulberry Street</u>
•separate signs for Home, School, and Mulberry St.
•five laminated pictures from <u>And to Think That I Saw It on Mulberry Street</u>:
Marco with the horse and wagon
Marco with a zebra
a reindeer
a blue elephant
a brass band
•five cones or posts
•optional: stop watch

Set up
•Place five cones in a row with enough room in between for weaving in and out.
•Place the signs for home and school at opposite ends of the arena.
•Place the Mulberry St. sign near the row of cones or posts.
•Place one picture on each cone or post in the order listed above.

Skills
•riding: steering, walk on, whoa, trotting, reverse turn
•following directions
•gross/fine motor skills
•problem solving
•sequencing

Introduction to the game
At meet and greet, ask who knows Dr. Seuss. Certainly some discussion of favorite books can follow. Dr. Seuss was born on March 2, 1904, and wrote forty-four children's books. Today the game acts out one of those stories.

During stretches, pretend to drive a wagon, have antlers like a reindeer, wave your trunk like an elephant, and play different instruments in a brass band.

At game time
Riders gather at the home sign. Riders weave in and out of the cones, collecting the items on the cones. At the school sign, turn around and ride straight home. More advanced riders can trot back home from school. Time the event if appropriate. Tell the story together using the pictures. Share the book.

The Iditarod

For this game the arena becomes a large board game representing the trip from Anchorage to Nome. Riders draw cards and follow the directions on the cards.

Equipment needed
•large cards with checkpoint names (one per card) as follows: Anchorage, Yneta Station, Rainy Pass, Iditarod, Eagle Island, Safety, Nome
•laminated photo of a sled dog team for each rider to carry or tape to saddle pad
•map of the Iditarod route to hang in the arena, available at www.iditarod.com
•set of file cards with "instructions" as follows:

>   --Dogs excited! Trot to next checkpoint.
>   --Moose on trail.   Lose one turn.
>   --One of your dogs is tired. Walk to next checkpoint.
>   --Slept really well last night in your tent. Trot ahead 2 checkpoints.
>   --Vet says your dogs need to rest. Lose 1 turn.
>   --Full moon. Trot ahead 2 checkpoints.
>   --Very cold temperatures. Walk to next checkpoint.
>   --Dogs very happy. Trot ahead 2 checkpoints.
>   --One dog lame. Walk slowly to next checkpoint
>   --Sun is out, snow is soft. Walk to next checkpoint.
>   --Wind at your back. Trot to next checkpoint.
>   --Snow is well packed. Trot to next checkpoint
>   --White out! Lose your way. Go back one checkpoint.
>   --Beautiful day. Trot ahead one checkpoint.
>   --Dogs lost booties. Walk back one checkpoint.
>   --Chased by wolves. Trot ahead 2 checkpoints.

Set up
•Place the checkpoint cards around the perimeter of the arena, equal distances apart.
•Hang the Iditarod map in the arena.
•Have the file cards and photos of dog teams handy.

Skills
•riding: walk on, whoa, trotting, steering, keeping proper distance from other horses, standing still
•following directions
•reading
•taking turns
•patience
•competition

Introduction to the game:
At meet and great, ask who has heard of the Iditarod. In 1925 during a diphtheria epidemic in Nome, serum was transported by train and dog sled from Anchorage to Nome. The first true Iditarod dogsled race over the historic trail was in 1973.

The Iditarod always begins the first Saturday in March with a "ceremonial" start in Anchorage. The official start site is farther north and varies year to year. The race ends in nine to fifteen days in Nome. It is about 1,150 miles. There is a southern route followed in odd-numbered years and a northern route used in even-numbered years. You will see some of the checkpoints around the arena. You need to be very strong to be a dogsled racer, so today during stretches do lots of "strength" stretches and flex your muscles!

At game time
Riders meet at the Anchorage checkpoint sign. Each rider gets a dogsled team and attaches it to his or her saddle. The instructor decides who draws a card first. Riders in turn draw a card and follow the instructions. The winner is the one who arrives in Nome first, but everyone completes the course.

....

Shamrock Races
This game is modified barrel racing with the riders learning a bit about St. Patrick.

Equipment needed
•three barrels or posts (I use posts with green cones on top.)
•three cutouts of shamrocks
•diagram of the barrel racing pattern. Here's one with a shamrock: http://blackjackdtc.blogspot.com/2011_01_01_archive.html
•optional Irish blessings to hand out:
"May the blessings outnumber the shamrocks that grow,
And may trouble avoid you wherever you go."
•small picture of a leprechaun
•stopwatch if you want to time the races

Set up
•Put shamrocks on the barrels or posts and arrange them in a triangle.
•Hang the diagram of the barrel racing pattern in the arena.
•Hide the leprechaun in the arena.

Skills
•riding: walk on, steering, trotting
•taking turns
•memory
•competition

Introduction to the game
At meet and greet, ask if anyone knows who celebrates Saint Patrick's Day and why. Saint Patrick is the patron saint of Ireland. He was born in Britain, captured and taken to Ireland at age sixteen as a slave, escaped and joined the church. Eventually he went back to Ireland as a missionary. The legend is that he banished all snakes from Ireland. He used the shamrock to teach about the Holy Trinity.

Leprechauns are in Irish folk lore and enjoy making mischief. If you find the one hiding in the arena, you will have good luck all year.

During stretches trace the outline of a shamrock in the air, pretend you are shooing the snakes out of the arena, and pretend to eat a big bowl of potatoes.

This is a good day to practice serpentines during the lesson in honor of Saint Patrick.

At game time
Riders take turns riding the race pattern at a walk with trotting back from the last barrel to the finish line. More advanced riders may want to trot the entire pattern. Don't forget to have the riders search for the leprechaun. At the end of the lesson pass out the Irish blessings.

••••••••••••••••

Ice Fishing
This is a homemade version of some of those plastic "fishing" games, with the added elements of what one really needs to go ice fishing.

Equipment needed
•two laminated pictures of local fish per rider, with pipe cleaner loops at the mouth
•a fishing license for your state (card that says "State of Maine Fishing License" for example) for each rider
•a picture of an auger for each rider
•a picture of a lure for each rider
•one fishing pole per rider: Kwiktwist with a turned up "hook" at one end works well.
(Another option is to use a child's toy magnetic fishing set)
•one barrel per rider upon which to place the fish
•one bucket per rider

Set up
•Place one barrel per rider in the arena with two (or more) fish on the barrel, pipe cleaner loops sticking up.
•Place fishing licenses, augurs, and lures around the arena within reach of riders.
•Place one pole on each barrel.
•Place buckets at the opposite end of the arena from the barrels.

Skills
•riding: walk on, steering, whoa, standing still
•small and large motor skills
•sequencing
•problem solving

Introduction to the game
At meet and greet, ask who has been ice fishing. You might discuss what you need to ice fish, so that riders can be on the lookout for these items during the lesson. During stretches, turn the augur to drill the hole in the ice, reel up the fishing line. No casting for ice fishing! Clean, cook, and eat the fish.

At Game time
Riders meet in the center of the arena. Each rider must pick up a fishing license, augur, and lure before going to the barrel and picking up the pole. The rider then tries to pick up the fish. Once the fish are caught, the rider proceeds to the bucket and places the fish in the bucket. Everyone wins.

•••••••••••••••••

Build an Igloo
In this game riders will collect the parts of an igloo and learn how an igloo is built. Riders will work on riding circles, as igloos are built by laying down blocks of snow in circles.

Equipment needed
•four posts
•one set of cards per rider, drawings or pictures of:
>>--a block of snow
>>--the tunnel leading into the igloo
>>--the igloo with about two rounds of blocks
>>--the lamp used inside

Use these web sites for pictures and information: http://en.wikipedia.org/wiki/Igloo and http://en.wikipedia.org/wiki/Kudlik
•a diagram of the side view of an igloo
•a picture of the lamp used in an igloo
•a photo of a completed igloo

Set up
•Place one post in each corner of the arena.
•On each post, place all of one of the igloo parts cards or all the lamp cards. There are four different cards, and four different posts.
•Hang the igloo photo, the lamp photo, and the diagram of the igloo in the arena.

Skills
•riding: walk on, whoa, standing still, riding circles, steering, keeping proper distance from other horses
•gross/fine motor skills
•sequencing
•following directions
•communication

Introduction to the game
At meet and greet, give some information on igloos and tell riders to look for the visuals around the arena.

Igloos are made with blocks of snow mostly by the Inuit in Canada's central Arctic region. There are three types of igloos: small and temporary for hunting, medium-sized for a family house, and large with two large parts for community feasts. The dome can support a person standing on the top. There is a special stone lamp used inside. Igloos are built in a spiral, so today riders will be working on circles.

During stretching, circle arms backwards, slowly, one arm then the other. Saw blocks of snow from the ice and snow. Stack blocks of snow.

At game time
Riders gather in the center of the arena. Show riders the photos of the igloo, diagram, and lamp. Each rider will go to a post and circle it, pick up the piece of the igloo, ride to the next post and do the same. When all four items have been picked up, riders return to the center. Riders will put the pieces in logical sequence: block of snow, igloo with two rounds, tunnel, and lamp for inside.

Games for April

April Fools'!
Black Fly Frenzy
Mud Season Madness
Peter Rabbit Obstacle Course
An Hawaiian Rodeo

April Fools'!

This game puts a surprising twist on some familiar activities (weaving cones, tossing bean bags) as well as introducing a French custom for the day.

Equipment needed
• lightweight posts with cones on top (four or five)
• bean bags, four per rider
• hula hoops, one per rider
• paper fish about palm size, with tape on back (Florescent file cards work nicely.)

Set up
• Place the lightweight posts with cones on top in a row with room to "weave" in and out.
• Place the hula hoops in the arena.
• Place the beanbags inside the hula hoops, on the ground.
• Hide one or more paper fish in your palm.

Skills
• riding: walk on, whoa, steering
• gross motor skills
• focus
• sense of humor!

Introduction to the game
When you are getting helmets on riders or when you are mounting riders, try to secretly get a paper fish on the rider's back or helmet.

At meet and greet, ask if anyone knows the origin of playing jokes on April first. It has to do with the change in the calendar around 1582 in France when New Year's Day was moved from the week of March 25 -- April 1 to January 1. Some people refused to make the change to January 1, continued to celebrate New Year's Day on April 1, and were called April Fools. Today in France, Sweden, and Italy, it is the custom to try and hang an "April Fish" on someone. It is the naive fish which is easily caught. Is anyone wearing a fish today?

On April 1,1998, Burger King advertised the Left-Handed Whopper in USA Today with a full page ad. What was your best April Fools' joke?

During stretches, you might "go fishing." Use the posts for steering practice in the "normal" way during the lesson.

At game time:
Meet at the posts. Let one rider at a time ride through the posts and see how many posts he/she can knock down (carefully) with a foot (no hands!). Check before the lesson to see if the horses can tolerate this. Our riders just love this game. The one who knocks down the most posts after one trip through, wins.

Proceed to the hula hoops. Each rider gets four bean bags and throws them with his eyes closed toward the hula hoop, but trying to miss. The one with the most bean bags outside the hoop wins.

Black Fly Frenzy

This game involves riding an obstacle course, "swatting" a black fly, learning a fact about black flies, and returning to a starting point.

Equipment needed
•one barrel for each rider
•two posts for each rider
•one traffic cone for each rider
•one fly swatter for each rider
•one photo of a giant black fly from the internet, laminated, hung on a string, hung from a Kwiktwist
•optional: one or more black fly nets for head
•a different fact card for each rider, laminated, clipped to a foam tab and hung on a post, facts as follows:

>--Black flies like dark colors: blue, purple, brown, and black. Wear light colors to avoid being bitten.
>--Black flies do not come indoors, and they do not fly at night.
>--There are 1,800 species of black flies! Males feed on nectar, and females feed on the blood of mammals and birds.
>--Black flies are attracted to the carbon dioxide in our breath.

Set up
•For each rider place a traffic cone near A as the starting point.
•Place a barrel opposite the traffic cone near C.
•Tape a Kwiktwist to the side of the barrel with a photo of a black fly hanging from a string. The photo should be able to swing on the string.
•In between the traffic cone and the barrel, place two posts, equally spaced.
•On the first post attach a fact card. There are many ways you can do this. One idea is to place a small cone over the top of the post, place a doorknob tab over that, and use a clothespin to attach the card to the doorknob tab.
•On the second post attach or hang a fly swatter. Hang the swatter over the top of a cone, or use a Kwiktwist to make a hook.

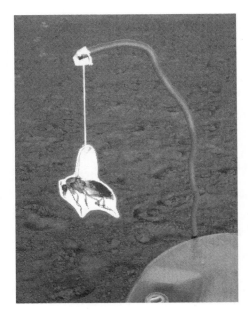

Skills
•riding: walk on, whoa, trotting
•reading,
•gross/fine motor skills
•balance
•memory
•following directions
•directionality

Introduction to the game

At meet and greet, show the riders the black fly net. Explain that black flies breed in running water, which is different from mosquitoes which breed in still water, and this makes them harder to control. For stretches have riders swim, fly, and swat flies.

At game time

Each rider begins standing to the left of a traffic cone, facing the barrel with the black fly. The instructor or a volunteer should walk this course to demonstrate the following directions. At "go", ride to the first post, staying to the right of the post. Whoa. Pick up the fact card and read it (Alternately, the volunteer may read it). Replace the fact card. Ride to the next post, staying to the left of the post. Whoa. Pick up the fly swatter. Ride to the barrel, keeping to the right of the barrel. Whoa. GENTLY swat/tap the fly. Circle around the barrel, keeping the barrel on the left. Ride back to the post where the fly swatter was. Keep left. Whoa. Hang the fly swatter back on the post. From here trot straight back to the traffic cone. When all riders arrive back at the cones, share the fact that was on the card, with help as necessary. Let the winner take a victory lap wearing the fly mask. Or, have one fly mask for each rider on hand so all can ride in a fly mask!

....

Mud Season Madness

This game is a glorified obstacle course with a pothole theme and a boot-carrying element.

Equipment needed

•hula hoops, two for each rider, to represent pot holes
•a boot for each rider, preferably a nice, dirty mud boot
•a small, plastic ring for each rider which will fit over the toe of the boot
•ground poles, one per rider, to represent ruts
•a barrel for each rider, upon which to place a boot and a ring
•a post for each rider which will mark the beginning and end of the course, and over which the rider will place the boot

Set up

•Set one upright post near A in the arena for each rider as a starting and ending point.
•Place a ground pole as a "rut" between A and C for each rider.
•Place two (or more) hula hoops as "pot holes" for each rider.
•Place a barrel near C with a boot and ring on top for each rider, in line with the starting post.

Skills

•riding: walk on, steering, whoa, back up, standing still
•problem solving (How do you carry a boot and steer at the same time?)
•following directions
•directionality
•gross motor skills

Introduction to the game

During meet and greet, talk about what makes mud, ways to deal with it, why we need the water, etc. (The top layer of soil melts but the water cannot drain down into the frozen ground beneath.) During stretches, do "mud swimming," pick up feet as if stuck in mud, drive a car through mud (thumbs up!), roll in the mud like a horse.

At game time
Line riders up at the posts facing the barrels. Riders must always keep to the right of the barrels to keep from turning into each other. The instructor or a volunteer walks the course to demonstrate.

At "go", riders must get to the barrel without clanking a "rut" or stepping into a pot hole, pick up a boot and ride back to the post. Riders must place the boot upside down over the top of the post.

Next, riders turn around the post, ride back through the mud course, and pick up the ring. Finally, riders return to the post and put the ring over the tip of the upside down boot. Each rider must turn the horse around and be in starting position to be "finished." (The rider may need to back up.) Riders could lose points for "clanking" the "ruts" or stepping in the "pot holes." Use your own judgment on how competitive you want this to be, or if you make it through the course without being sucked into the "mud," YOU WIN! Modify as necessary.

....

Peter Rabbit Obstacle Course
This obstacle course takes riders through Mr. McGregor's Garden.

Equipment needed
•four ground poles
•four posts with cones on top
•three separate photos of vegetables Peter eats: lettuce, radishes, green beans
•drawing of Peter's jacket
•sign saying HOME
•helpful if instructor knows the story of Peter Rabbit, copy of book is optional
•optional stop watch

Set up
•Place four ground poles at B, parallel to the side rail.
•Place each vegetable photo on a cone, and place each cone on a post.
•Place Peter's jacket on a cone which is on a post.
•Line up the "vegetable" posts from X to C, with Peter's jacket on the post nearest C.
•Place the HOME sign near K.
•Have the stop watch handy.

Skills
•riding: two-point, walk on, whoa, steering, trotting
•listening
•gross motor skills

Introduction to the game

At meet and greet, ask who knows the story of Peter Rabbit. Tell riders they will be riding through Mr. McGregor's garden. During stretches the instructor may choose to tell the story of Peter Rabbit, with riders stretching to pull up a carrot, eating carrots, running away from Mr. McGregor (arm motions), sliding under the fence, hiding in the watering can, reaching up to pick blackberries.

At game time

Riders line up along the rail near B. Riders will go through the obstacle course one at a time, with timing at the instructor's discretion. Begin in two-point over the poles. Peter is sneaking under the fence. Next weave in and out of the vegetables, reaching to "pick" each vegetable. At the "scarecrow" (Peter's jacket), turn left and head straight for HOME at a trot if able, because Mr. McGregor is coming! Replace the vegetables for the next rider.

....

An Hawaiian Rodeo

This is four simple games with an Hawaiian theme.

Equipment needed

•Hawaiian music for background, if possible
•leis for riders and volunteers
•two plastic pink flamingos, each mounted on a post
•traffic cones
•hula hoop
•plastic pineapple, or beanie baby fish and tropical birds, or coconut
•palm trees (foam or made of poster paper) taped to posts or small traffic cones
•map of Hawaii
•multiple choice fact file cards as follows:

   --Aloha means: Greetings!, Hello!, Goodbye!, all of these (yes)
   --Hawaii is surrounded by: the Atlantic Ocean, the Pacific Ocean (yes), Sebago Lake (put in a lake near where you live)
   --Hawaii has how many main islands? 8 (yes), 23, 42
   --Hawaii grows: pineapples (yes), blueberries, Christmas trees
   --Mahalo means: thank you (yes), you're welcome, see you soon
   --Hawaii was which number state? 10, 50 (yes), 37
   --The state animal of Hawaii is: the moose, the crocodile, the humpback whale   (yes)
   --Hawaii was formed by: bulldozers, earthquakes, volcanoes (yes)

Set up

•Place posts with palm trees in such a way that riders can make a figure 8 around them.
•Put the map of Hawaii somewhere in the arena.
•Put the hula hoop in the center of the arena, or anywhere that works for your set up.

•For flamingo pole bending, set the post with the flamingo at one end of the arena with leis hanging on it.
•Place three to five cones in line in front of the post with flamingo and leis, and another flamingo on a post at end of the line.

Skills
•riding: walk on, steering, whoa, trotting, standing still
•problem solving
•communication
•gross/fine motor skills
•following directions

Introduction to the game
During meet and greet, tell riders they are going to Hawaii today. This is a good game for a really cold winter day or a spring day when it just doesn't seem to get warm. Pass out leis to all riders and volunteers. Teach the word "mahalo" for thank you. For stretches, have riders surf, swim, climb a palm tree, do the hula, try to crack open a coconut, eat pineapple.

At game time
This "rodeo" has several events. Scoring is optional.

Hawaiian Trivia
Have riders find the map of Hawaii and ride to it. Ask the question cards, gaining points for correct answers.

Palm Tree Figure 8
Have riders ride a figure 8 around the palm trees, making fat, round 8s.

Pineapple Toss (or tropical fish or coconut, depending on what you can get, or what you prefer)
The rider is beside the hula hoop, the distance away at the instructor's discretion. The hula hoop is to the side of the rider so that the pineapple is tossed to the side, not over the horse's head. The rider tosses the pineapple into the hoop. Try this as many tries as it takes, adjusting distance as necessary, until the rider succeeds.

Flamingo Pole Bending
The rider picks up a lei at the post, puts it over his or her arm, weaves in and out of the cones, goes around the flamingo, stopping to put the lei on the flamingo's neck, and trots straight back to the beginning. This is a good event to time, but it's not necessary.

Be sure at the end of the lesson that each rider says "Mahalo" to the volunteers and horses. Leis may be awarded as prizes to all.

Games for May

Hiking the Appalachian Trail

This is designed to be done outside on a trail, but can be done in an arena. Riders follow the Appalachian Trail blazes or symbol and learn about the Trail.

Equipment needed
Each of the following "blazes" should be laminated and have string at the top to hang on a tree if you are using it outside.

•small map of the Appalachian Trail with the following information on back:
A thru-hiker does the whole trail in one season. In 1948 Earl Shaffer completed the first thru-hike, south to north. Later Shaffer completed the first north to south thru-hike. In 1998 Mr. Shaffer, nearly eighty years old, again hiked the whole trail, making him the oldest person ever to complete a thru-hike.
•white "blaze" 2" x 6" with the following on the back: This is the size and shape of an AT blaze, used to mark the trail.
The following "blazes" can be made using the AT symbol, with the information on the back, or they can be white blaze size and shape.
•It takes about 5 million footsteps to walk the length of the trail.
•The AT is marked by about 165,000 blaze marks, white rectangles 2" by 6". Blue rectangles mark side paths.
•Maine's 281 miles of the trail are especially difficult. More moose are seen by hikers in Maine than in any other state on the trail. The end of the trail is on Mount Katahdin in Maine's Baxter State Park.
•The AT runs 2,178 miles from Georgia to Maine. It is the nation's longest footpath.
•The AT touches fourteen states.
•The AT was the idea of Benton MacKaye, a forester, in 1921. The AT was completed in 1937.

Set up
If you are going on a trail ride, simply hang the "blazes" along the trail you are going to take. Have riders watch for the next blaze.

If you are going to do this inside, then place the blazes anywhere around the arena.

Skills
•riding: trail riding, steering, whoa, standing still
•reading
•listening
•looking

Introduction to the game
If you are going out on the trail, at meet and greet, tell everyone that today's adventure is a "hike" on the Appalachian Trail and proceed to the trail map which is hanging outside.

If you are riding inside, at meet and greet, ask who has heard of the AT and tell riders they will be looking for blazes to learn about the trail. During stretches have them put a hand to the forehead and stretch the neck forward "looking", or look with pretend binoculars. Pretend to walk with a hiking stick, put on the back pack, drink from a water bottle.

At game time
If you are outside, simply proceed from blaze to blaze, stopping to read the information, noticing things in your environment, and talking about hiking.

If you are inside, the game is to search for each blaze and read the information.

....

What Good Is a Tree?
This game sparks the imagination, teaches about trees, and is a variation of egg and spoon.

Equipment needed
•two Brazil nuts per rider
•optional but really nice: a copy of Karen I. Shragg's poem "Think Like a Tree" at: http://www.spiritoftrees.org/poetry/shragg/think_tree_shragg.html
•several photos from the internet of interesting trees, for example, a baobab tree, Brazil nut tree, tallest tree, oldest tree, and especially one of the Brazil nut tree seed pod.
•one large plastic spoon per rider
•one plastic bucket per rider

Set up
•Place photos of various trees around the arena.
•Have buckets, spoon, and Brazil nuts handy in arena.

Skills
•riding: one-handed reining, walk on, steering
•communication
•creativity
•gross/fine motor skills

Introduction to the game
Before riders mount, if they are able, have them attempt the yoga "Tree Pose." Modify as necessary, perhaps on two feet instead of one. At meet and greet, read the poem "Think Like a Tree," if you choose. Ask riders, "What good is a tree?" Ask riders, "What good is a horse?" Ask riders, "How is a tree like a horse?"

Characteristics of a tree: It is a perennial with an upright trunk at least 3" in diameter. It is at least 13 feet tall with a crown of leaves.
Stretches: leaves falling, swaying in the wind, branches growing, climbing a tree, building a tree fort, sliding down a tree trunk.

At game time
Have riders search for pictures of trees around the arena, ride to each one, and talk about them. (The Brazil nut tree can grow to 150' and has yellow flowers with a sweet nectar. The baobab can live thousands of years. The giant sequoia can grow to nearly 280 feet.) Have riders imitate

an Oak tree, a weeping willow tree, an evergreen tree. Riders meet at A where the buckets, spoons, and nuts are. This is essentially "egg and spoon," but with Brazil nuts instead. Each rider must carry the nuts in the spoon to the other end of the arena and back, then get the nuts into the bucket.

Another activity to go with this theme is to create a poster of all the answers to the questions asked during meet and greet. Volunteers enjoy joining in on this, too.

Feet!
Modified horseshoes and facts about human and horse feet comprise this game.

Equipment needed
•side view drawing of a horse's lower leg, cannon bone to hoof
•bottom view drawing of a horse's hoof
•side view drawing of a human foot from below the knee
•"horseshoes" made from Kwiktwists, two Kwiktwists per shoe, one "horseshoe" per rider This makes for a soft, quiet horseshoe for tossing.
•one post per rider
•optional: a metal horse shoe to show

Set up
•Place the drawings of human and horse feet in the arena, in the same area. A white board is very handy for this.
•Place the posts in the center of the arena forming a line between B and E, with "horse shoes" leaning on them.

Skills
•riding: walk on, steering, whoa, standing still
•gross motor skills
•hand/eye coordination
•communication

Introduction to the game
At meet and greet, ask riders, "How is a horse's foot like a human foot? How is a horse's foot different from a human foot?" During stretches be sure to wiggle the feet, make circles with the feet, point the toes down, point the toes up.

At game time
Have riders meet at the foot pictures. How many bones are in a horse's foot? (6) How many bones are in a human foot? (26). Point out that the hoof is like a finger nail. Compare the drawings. Show parts of the bottom of a horse hoof. Ask if anyone knows when horseshoes were invented. (In the 6th and 7th centuries there were metal shoes.) Current thinking is that metal shoes are bad for the horse because they prevent the wall from flexing near the heel. The flexing action pulls blood into the hoof. Shoes contract the hoof. The frog acts as a shock absorber, but cannot do that when a shoe is present. Shock absorption is lost. It is estimated

that a gallon of blood is pumped up in twenty strides. There are no muscles in the lower leg or hoof to pump the blood. The frog relates to the human finger tip.

Each rider has a post and a "horseshoe." According to ability, riders will toss the horseshoe, not over the horse's head, and try to ring the post. Instructors make up appropriate scoring. (Ringers, leaners, etc.)

················

Thar She Blows!

This game focuses on the sizes of whales and collecting "food" for them. Riders ride the length of various whales, learn about whales, then play "musical whales," a variation of musical stalls.

Equipment needed
•four posts
•50 or 100 foot long measuring tape
•photo of krill, one per rider, plus one
•photo of inside of a baleen whale's mouth showing the baleen
•photo of each of the following whales with information on back:
    --orca: 20 to 26 feet, 6 tons, eats herring, seals, other fish, eats 500 lbs per day, has teeth
    --minke: 30 feet, 10 tons, eats small schooling fish, herring, cod, has baleen, no teeth
    --humpback: 40 to 60 feet, 40 tons, eats herring, mackerel, cod, krill, has baleen
    --blue: largest living creature on earth, 90 plus feet, 110 tons, eats krill
•Label each of the above whale species with its name on the front.
•CD with whale songs, if possible, or "nautical" music

Set up
•Starting from A and heading toward C, mark off 20' and put a post with the orca whale photo. At 30' put a post with the minke whale photo. At 50' put a post with the humpback whale photo. At 90' put a post with the blue whale photo. This shows the students the sizes of the 4 species of whales.
•"Hide" photos of krill in the arena, one photo per rider. Keep one photo to show riders what they are looking for. Note that the largest whale eats the smallest food.
•Have the photo of baleen handy.

Skills
•riding: walk on, whoa, steering, keeping proper distance from other horses
•listening
•competition
•sensory integration

Introduction to the game
At meet and greet, ask riders what they know about whales. Ask if they know what is or was the largest living animal on earth. (Many think a dinosaur, but it's the blue whale.) Show riders how the posts are arranged and tell them which whales are represented. During stretches riders should open their mouths wide to gulp for fish and krill, flap their arms the way humpbacks do, dive, hold their breath, and let their breath out with a whoosh.

At game time

Riders meet at A and ride toward C. Each rider stops at each cone to look at the photo of the whale and read or listen to the facts about the whale. After each whale has been identified, each rider is sent out to look for a krill card. Riders return to X, meeting the instructor. Each rider then chooses a different whale and rides to it. The instructor puts on whale songs or other music reminiscent of the sea. When the music stops, each rider rides to his or her own particular whale. Play as many times as interest or time allows. It's "musical whales," and everyone wins.

·················

Reach for the Stars

This game is all about steering through a pattern of "stars," learning a bit about stars, riding to music, and sharing dreams.

Equipment needed
•seven posts
•seven cardboard star shapes
•"Star Wars" music, Gustav Holst's "The Planets," or other "celestial " music.
•a set of cards with a question on the front and the answer on the back as follows:
>--What is the nearest star? the sun
>--What is a star? a ball of gas that releases energy
>--What is the brightest star? Sirius (the Dog Star), = to 20 of our suns
>--What is a comet? frozen gas and dust, remains from the outer planets. Comets orbit the sun and have a tail made of dust.
>--Which state has the Big Dipper on its flag? Alaska
>--Where is the North Star located? directly over the North Pole
>--Why do some people put a star on top of their Christmas tree? It represents the star of Bethlehem.

•star dust

Set up
•Place the posts in the shape of the Big Dipper, with 3 for the handle and 4 for the bowl.
•Place one star card on top of each post.
•music: "Star Wars" or Holst's "the Planets" or music of your choice

Skills
•riding: walk on, steering, whoa
•sensory integration
•communication
•listening
•gross motor skills
•reading
•speaking
•memory

Introduction to the game

At meet and greet, ask if anyone ever looks at the stars. Ask riders if they know of any constellations. Ask riders if they know what shape the posts are in. Ask riders if they understand the expression "reach for the stars." Ask riders to think about their goals, hopes, dreams, aspirations for sharing later. During stretches, be sure to reach for the stars. Draw a star in the air as you ride. Throw star dust all around.

During the lesson, weave in and out of the stars in the Big Dipper.

At game time

Have riders ride to the last star in the handle of the Big Dipper. Depending on the number of riders, riders may proceed individually through the stars, stopping to read the question privately, or riders may move as a group, sharing the information. At each post/star, the rider reaches for the star, reads the question and attempts an answer. Rider or volunteer or instructor reads the answer. After all riders have ridden through the stars, whoa, and ask who can remember one fact about stars. Share aspirations and stretch up as tall as possible. Put on the "Star Wars" music and ride through the stars one more time.

Games for June

Thunderstorms

In this game, riders learn about safe activities during different types of weather. Riders choose weather cards and must ride to a picture of a safe activity or safe place.

Equipment needed

Make a set of cards with a picture on the front and the information on the back.
- drawings or photos of
  - --a house -- You are generally safe in a house during a thunderstorm. Close the windows.
  - --a car -- You are generally safe in a car during a thunderstorm. Close the windows.
  - --an umbrella -- During a thunderstorm do not hold anything that would attract lightning: golf clubs, metal bat, tools, umbrella.
  - --a TV -- Do not use the TV or other appliances during a thunderstorm.
  - --a swimming pool -- Get out of the pool or lake or ocean. If you are in a small boat, get to shore and get off the water. Also, get out of the tub.
  - --a tree -- Do not stand under a lone tree during a thunderstorm.
- drawings or photos of three different thunderstorm scenes with the facts listed below
  - --At any given time 2,000 thunderstorms are happening around the world.
  - --In a typical thunderstorm, the amount of energy released is about equal to the amount of energy used by a city of 100,000 people for a month.
  - --To figure out how far away a thunderstorm is in miles, count the seconds after the lightning until you hear the thunder, then divide by 5.
- drawings or photos of the sun (a sunny day) and the sun with clouds (a cloudy day)

Set up
- Place the house, car, umbrella, TV, pool, and tree cards randomly around the arena.
- Hold on to the weather cards.

Skills
- riding: walk on, steering, whoa, standing still, trotting
- listening
- reasoning

Introduction to the game
At meet and greet, ask riders what they know about thunderstorms. Tell them they will be playing a game about what to do in a thunderstorm. Tell them to notice the pictures around the arena during the lesson. During stretches, riders should make it rain and use their arms to make wind and thunder. Cover their heads in the rain. Crouch down low beside the neck of the horse to get out of the weather, or try two-point.

At game time
Riders meet with the instructor in the center of the arena. Each rider chooses a weather card from the instructor. Read the cards with writing. If there is no writing, decide what the picture means. When the instructor says "go", each rider moves to a picture which represents a safe activity during the weather on the card chosen. Check the back of the picture card to see if the rider is correct. If the rider is not correct, have the rider find a safe place. Trot back to the center

for the next round. Depending on the number of riders, play a few rounds, mixing the cards so that all get used.

••••••••••••••

The Triple Crown
In this game riders choose a race horse and "race" one at a time to win the Triple Crown.

Equipment needed
•three file cards: Secretariat (1973), Seattle Slew (1977), and Affirmed (1978)
(These are the most recent winners as of this publication.)
•stop watch or second hand on a watch
•optional: "Call to Post", the bugle call used before horse races, available on line

Set up
None, can you believe it? Clear the arena!

Skills
•riding: trotting in two-point, posting trot, sitting trot, or fast walk, as appropriate
•competition
•listening
•following instructions
•body awareness
•taking turns

Introduction to the game
At meet and greet, ask if anyone has heard of the Kentucky Derby, the Preakness, or the Belmont Stakes. Explain that any horse who wins all three races in five weeks has won the Triple Crown. The first winner was Sir Barton in 1919. There have been only eleven winners, as of 2012. Each race is a little longer than the previous one: 1 1/4 miles, 1 3/16 miles, and 1 1/2 miles. Each race is represented by a different flower: the rose for the Derby, the black-eyed Susan for the Preakness, and the carnation for the Belmont Stakes.

During stretches be sure and take a jockey's position (two point), then raise arms in victory. Smell the flowers!

At game time
Riders meet the instructor at A and will race one at a time in two point (or modified). All races go counter clockwise. Each rider chooses the name of a horse from the instructor's cards and puts the name on his saddle pad. Time each rider with a stopwatch and a flourish. Play the "Call to Post" before the race!

Why Is it Summer?

In this game, riders ride through the solar system (the whole arena) collecting symbols representing the seasons.

Equipment needed
•a chart explaining the changing seasons, for example the one at http://visual.merriam-webster.com/earth/meteorology/seasons-year.php
•a drawing or photo of the sun
•one set of season symbols for each rider. Starting with summer I used a tree in green leaves, a fall colored leaf, a snow flake, and a spring flower.
•one post

Set up
•Place the sun on a post, and place the post at X in the arena.
•Place all of the summer symbols at C, representing the summer solstice.
•Place all of the fall symbols at E, representing the fall equinox.
•Place all of the winter symbols at A, representing the winter solstice.
•Place all of the spring symbols at B, representing the spring equinox.
•Put the changing seasons chart up somewhere in the arena.

Skills
•riding: walk on, steering, whoa
•listening
•gross motor skills
•sequencing
•speaking

Introduction to the game
At meet and greet, ask riders what season it is now and what the seasons are. Tell riders they will ride through the seasons all the way around the sun, going through the solstices and equinoxes. In the summer, the earth in our hemisphere tilts toward the sun so it is warmer. At the equinoxes day and night are equal length. During stretches, invent ways to show each season; for example, shivering in winter or wiping sweat away in summer, smelling flowers in spring, and raking leaves in the fall.

At game time
Show riders the diagram of the changing seasons and point out that the arena is set up to look like that. Riders will circle the arena collecting the four symbols of the seasons. Each rider chooses a different season, beginning at either A, B, C, or E, and rides to that season. Then each rider completes the circle. When all riders have completed the ride through the seasons, riders report to "the sun" at X and show/share their season cards. Riders say the seasons in order. Everyone wins.

A Cattle Drive on the Chisholm Trail

This is a game to be used on a trail ride.

Equipment needed

•Make one set of six laminated cards, with a photo of a longhorn steer on the front and questions and facts as listed below on the back. Put a string on the top of each card for hanging it in a tree on the trail.

--What is a cattle drive? Cattle move from where they are raised to railheads where they are shipped east. The cattle walk on the cattle drive. Cowboys move them forward.

--What was the most famous trail for moving cattle? The Chisholm Trail, from various locations in Texas to Abilene, Kansas, was 1,000 miles long.

--How far did they go each day, and what did they eat? They travelled 10 to 15 miles a day. The cows ate grass, and the men ate bread, meat, beans, bacon and coffee. The men were paid $40 per month.

--When were the most famous cattle drives? During 1866 to 1886 over 20 million cattle were moved from Texas to Kansas.

--Who went on a cattle drive? One boss, 10 to 15 hands, each with 5 to 10 horses (called a remuda, Spanish for change of horses), one horse wrangler, one cook, and 1,500 to 2,500 head of cattle went on the drive.

--Are there cattle drives today? Yes! Most drives today are in Nevada. There are also drives for tourists.

Set up

•Walk through your trail ride and hang the longhorn cattle in trees along the trail.

Skills

riding: riding on a trail, walk on, whoa
•concentration
•listening

Introduction to the game

At meet and greet, tell the riders they are going on a cattle drive on the famous Chisholm Trail. Tell them they will have to look for cattle along the way. Stretches include packing their saddle bags, looking for longhorn cattle, roping, and throwing a rope.

At game time

Ride from sign to sign asking the questions and discussing the answers. Happy trails!

••••••••••••••••

Rainforests

This is a good game for a rainy summer day. The arena becomes a giant game board, and the riders ride through the various layers of a rainforest.

Equipment needed

•5 cards to place in the arena with the information listed below on the front
--forest floor -- decaying stuff!

--understory -- birds, snakes, lizards, jaguars, leopards

--canopy -- eagles, bats, monkeys, insects

--emergent -- eagles, bats, monkeys, butterflies

--drawing or picture of the sun

•one set of T/F game cards as follows:

--It only takes 30 seconds for rain to reach the forest floor from the emergent layer.   F It can take 20 minutes.

--In Asian rainforests there are flying frogs, squirrels, and snakes.   T

--50,000 tribal people live in rain forests.   F 50,000,000

--1,000 species go extinct each year due to cutting down rain forests. F 50,000

--Rainforests cover 10% of the earth's surface.   F less than 2%

--1 out of 4 ingredients in all medicines comes from rainforests.   T

--Giant bamboo can grow 2 feet per day in a rainforest.   F 9" per day

--One of the wettest places on earth is on Kauai. It gets 400" of rain per year. T

--Rainforests are called the earth's lungs because they produce oxygen.   T

--Every second a slice of rainforest the size of a football field is mowed down. T

--Trees in the emergent layer can be up to 240' tall. T

--Rainforests regulate temperatures and weather patterns world wide. T

--Rainforests have at least 100" of rain per year. F 68" to 78"

--Rainforests are found on every continent. F not on Antarctica

--Maine usually gets about 3.5" of rain in June. T (Check your own state's rainfall.)

--Lumber, coffee, cocoa, and plants to treat cancer all grow in the rain forest. T

•optional: If you have a collection of beanie babies or stuffed toys, put any that appear in a layer of the rainforest at the appropriate card.

Set up
•Place the five cards representing the layers of the rainforest spaced equally around the arena in order from the forest floor to the sun: floor, understory, canopy, emergent, sun.

•Have the T/F cards in your pocket.

Skills
•riding: walk on, whoa, standing still

•listening

•speaking

•counting

Introduction to the game
At meet and greet, tell riders they will be visiting a rainforest. You may investigate what riders already know about rainforests. During stretches, riders should make it rain, be a snake, eagle, bat, monkey, butterfly, leopard.

At game time
Riders meet at the rainforest floor sign, lining up side by side. The object is to work your way up through the layers of the rainforest (ride around the arena) by answering true/false questions. For a correct answer the rider rides half way to the next level. For an incorrect answer, the instructor tells the rider how many steps to take. (Not as far as half way, obviously. Each rider should always move ahead, and counting steps is an excellent exercise.) This can be modified

as necessary, and volunteers can also help with answers. Ride until all riders have made it to the sun. At the end, have riders share one fact they have learned about the rainforest.

Games for July

The Unbirthday Party

This is a take off on pin the tail on the donkey. It is a way of celebrating everyone's birthday and our country's birthday.

Equipment needed
•a laminated drawing of a donkey with no tail (Some discount stores have pin the tail on the donkey games.)
•several "tails" for the donkey (laminated paper or yarn or bailing twine)
•a birthday cake poster
•candles made of construction paper or cardboard, one per rider and volunteer, personalized or generic
•masking tape on the back of tails and candles
•bandana for loosely covering eyes (modify as necessary, perhaps just close eyes)
•optional -- small calendar and pen in your pocket in which to write down birthdays for future reference, and "party favors" of some sort, such as stickers or erasers, or small flags for the 4th of July

If you have a large, mounted white board in the arena you can draw the "cake" on that instead of making a paper one.

Set up
•Hang the donkey in the arena with a bandana near or on it.
•Place the tails around the arena on a rail within reach.
•Hang the "cake" in the arena.
•Place the candles around the arena on the rail within reach.

Skills
•riding: walk on, steering, whoa, standing still, taking turns
•communication
•gross motor skills
•trust (if blindfolded)
•social skills
•spatial relations

Introduction to the game
During meet and greet, ask each rider his/her birthday. (If you know the rider is unable to tell you his/her birthday, make sure you get it from the records.) Ask volunteers their birthdays also. Have each rider tell his/her favorite birthday present ever, or what he/she would like for the next birthday. Ask who knows the date of our country's birthday. During stretches, blow out candles, open presents, pop balloons, eat cake, wave flags.

At game time
Have each rider ride to a tail and pick it up, then come back to the donkey. Put the bandana (if appropriate) on the rider, and let him/her stick the tail on. Repeat with other riders. Closest tail gets lots of congratulations and cheers. Any tail anywhere on the donkey "wins!"

Have each rider find the candle with his/her name on it, with the help of a volunteer if necessary, pick it up and ride to the cake. Volunteers can also find candles with their names. Riders go to the cake one at a time and put the candles on. Sing happy unbirthday to "everybody." It might actually BE someone's birthday, which makes it even more fun. Sing "Yankee Doodle" for our country's birthday!

••••••••••••••••

Lis Hartel Day

This game helps us remember who was very influential in creating therapeutic riding. It is especially appropriate near the summer Olympics.

Equipment needed
•a photo of Lis Hartel on her horse Jubilee, can be found on the internet
•a print out of the Olympic flag
•five cones: blue, yellow, black, green, red, representing the colors of the Olympic rings
•five rings of the same colors.
(If you don't have exactly these colors you can use construction paper over the cones.)

Set up
•Place the cones in the arena in a line in the same order as they appear on the flag far enough apart so riders can weave in and out: blue, yellow, black, green, red
•Have the five rings handy.
•Place the photo of Lis Hartel in the arena.

Skills
•riding: walk on, steering, whoa
•listening
•following directions
•gross motor skills
•colors
•speaking

Introduction to the game
At meet and greet, ask riders if they know about equestrian events in the summer Olympics (dressage, three day eventing, show jumping). Be sure riders understand the work involved to be an Olympic rider. During stretches, give the victory sign, touch knees and toes if able, get into two-point, and think of other summer Olympic sports to imitate.

At game time
Riders meet the instructor at A. Show the riders the Olympic flag. The colors represent the colors in the flags of all countries. Show the riders the picture of Lis Hartel, a woman who lived in Denmark. She was a serious rider when, at the age of twenty-three, she got polio. This left her with no feeling in her legs from the knees down. Her doctors told her she could not ride, but for eight years, she worked at improving her riding. In 1952 she was one of the first women riders in the Olympics. She won the silver medal in dressage. Almost no one knew she had no feeling in her lower legs. The man who won the gold medal, Henri St Cyr, carried her to the podium to receive her medal. Four years later in Stockholm, she won the silver medal again.

She began Europe's first therapeutic riding center shortly after winning her first Olympic medal. Perhaps today we owe her a big thank you.

Each rider takes the five rings and places each one on the corresponding color cone. After each rider has done that, all riders ride a victory lap around the arena. All riders say thank you to Lis Hartel.

················

Misty of Chincoteague

This game acts out swimming the sound on Pony Penning Day from the story of Misty. Riders must earn enough coins to buy her by naming horse parts.

Equipment needed
•small stuffed horse to represent Misty, or the Breyer Misty, one for each rider
•two posts
•plastic coins
•a bucket
•optional: a copy of the book Misty of Chincoteague
•optional: have cards with drawings of parts of a horse, not labeled

Set up
•Place one post near A and the other post near C. These will represent the sound that Misty has to swim across.
•Place the bucket in the arena, it doesn't matter where.
•Have the coins in your pocket.
•Place the horses representing Misty near A.

Skills
•riding: walk on, two-point, whoa, standing still
•knowledge of horse parts
•speaking
•gross motor skills

Introduction to the game
At meet and greet, ask who has read Misty of Chincoteague. Explain that it is based on a true story about the wild horses on Assateague Island in Maryland and Virginia. There are about 300 protected horses there. On the Virginia side, on the last Wednesday of July, about 150 of the horses are rounded up. They swim at low tide across the sound, and the next day there is an auction to benefit the fire department. The story is about a brother and sister who want to buy a certain pony called "The Phantom". They have to earn money to buy her by doing chores. On Pony Penning Day, it is discovered that she has a foal, which the children name Misty. During the swim Misty needs help to stay afloat. Show pictures if you have the book.

During stretches, riders should do a lot of chores around the barn: hammering repairs, shoveling manure, dumping shavings, washing the windows.

At game time

Explain that the riders will earn coins to use to buy Misty. For each horse body part that they can name, they earn a coin. This can be done in many different ways, either by pointing to a part of the horse, or by showing a drawing of a horse part. Riders can also just name off parts and point. For each correct part, give the rider a coin. Coins are all placed/tossed in the bucket when this part of the game is done. Have a volunteer help count the coins.

Now the riders meet at the post near A and get ready to swim across the sound. Each rider holds a stuffed or plastic horse representing Misty, gets into two-point, and "swims" up the arena toward C. Let's hope everyone makes it across! This is not a race.

....

Making Hay while the Sun Shines

This game teaches riders how grass gets to the barn as hay. Riders collect pictures of the process and put them in the proper sequence.

Equipment needed

•one set of the following cards per rider:
> --a picture of the sun
> --a picture of a tractor mowing hay
> --a picture of a tractor tedding the hay into rows
> --a picture of a tractor bailing the hay
> --a picture of a barn

Set up

•All of the cards are placed randomly around the arena where the riders can reach them.

Skills

•riding: walk on, whoa, standing still, steering
•sequencing
•communication
•speaking
•gross motor skills

Introduction to the game

At meet and greet, ask riders if they know what the expression "Make hay while the sun shines" means. Explain. Ask riders where hay comes from. Many do not realize it is simply dried grasses and legumes. Explain the process of waiting for a sunny few days, mowing, tedding, bailing, and putting into the barn. During stretches riders should make a sun, cut the hay, ted it, bail it, and throw it into the barn.

At game time

Riders gather in the middle of the arena. All are instructed to find five different pictures, collect them, and return to the center of the arena. When they come back to the center, riders whoa and put the pictures in the proper sequence and tell about the process, as able.

Who Walked By?

In this game, riders will try to match pictures of tracks with pictures of animals. This game works well in winter with snow tracks, also.

Equipment needed
Choose four animals found in your area, including a horse. I used a horse, moose, rabbit, and turkey.
•a picture of each animal
•a picture of each animal's tracks.

Set up
•Place the four animal pictures around the arena.
•Keep the animal track pictures in your pocket.

Skills
•riding: walk on, whoa, steering
•reasoning
•communication
•gross motor skills

Introduction to the game
At meet and greet, tell riders to find the four animals in the arena as they ride. Tell them later they will be identifying the footprints they each leave. At stretching, imitate each animal.

At game time
Riders meet in the center of the arena. Give each rider a picture of an animal track. Tell riders to ride to the animal they believe made the track. Make corrections as necessary. Return to the center to return your track and get another. Play until everyone has matched the correct track with each animal.

Games for August

Seahorse Hunt

Riders will collect information about another kind of "horse" in this game.

Equipment needed

This game is designed for one, two, or three riders. The description provided is for three riders.

•three traffic cones
•three different colors of file cards, four of each color, explained below, with a seahorse picture on the back of each card

> first color card set:
>> --3,000 brine shrimp, one day's food
>> --Seahorses have great camouflage.
>> --Seahorses have no teeth.
>> --Male seahorses bear the young.
> second color card set:
>> --3,000 brine shrimp, one day's food
>> --Seahorses swim upright.
>> --Seahorses have no stomach.
>> --There are fifty-three species of seahorses.
> third color card set:
>> --3,000 brine shrimp, one day's food
>> --Seahorses are fish, but they are not great swimmers.
>> --Seahorses eat constantly.
>> --The fin on the back of a seahorse flutters up to 35 times per second.

Set up

•Place the three cones along the B side of the arena.
•Place one different color fact card on the top of each cone, but place the "3,000 brine shrimp card" elsewhere as explained below.
•Place the rest of the color cards as follows:

> --Along the A side, place the color cards that match the first cone.
> --Along the E side, place the cards that match the cone in the middle.
> --Along the C side, place the cards that match the cone closest to C.

This layout keeps riders from running into each other.

Skills

•riding: walk on, steering, whoa, keeping proper distance from other horses
•following directions
•gross motor skills
•reading
•memory
•communication

Introduction to the game

At meet and greet, tell the riders today they will learn about another type of "horse." Ask who has seen a seahorse or who knows something about a seahorse. Seahorses eat a lot, so during stretches make sure you eat a lot, and also try a lot of different swimming strokes.

At game time

Riders meet the instructor in the center of the arena. Each rider is assigned a color and rides to the cone with that color card on top. Pick up your seahorse and read the card. Each rider must find food for a day, and two other fact cards about seahorses. Read each card, and return to your starting cone. When all have finished have each rider or rider/volunteer team give at least one fact about seahorses.

••••••••••••••••

Going Batty!

The arena becomes a large board game. Riders must help their own bat get to the food by answering questions about bats and taking a certain number of steps.

Equipment needed
•various photos of bats, one per rider. suggestions: (all found on the internet)
    --Kitti's Hog-Nosed Bat, the smallest at just over an inch
    --baby flying fox bats wrapped in blankets
    --giant golden crown flying fox bat, the largest bat at three pounds with a wing span
    of nearly five feet -- This gets everyone's attention!
•a clothespin on each bat photo card for attaching it to the horse's mane
•bat cards as follows:
    --How long can bats live? 20 years
    --30% of all bats eat ---? fruit and nectar
    --Why should you NOT handle bats? They spread disease.
    --70% of all bats eat ---? insects
    --Why do bats hunt at night? They don't have to compete with birds.
    --How do bats see? The ones who eat insects use echolocation. The bats who eat fruit
    and nectar have very good eyes.
    --How are bats helpful? They pollinate flowers, spread fruit seeds and eat insects.
    --How many species of bats drink blood? There are 1,100 species of bats. Only
    three species drink blood!
    --Why do we think of bats at Halloween? They are symbols of ghosts, death,
    disease, and night.
    --How is a bat like a horse? They are both mammals. (and...?)
•photos of flowers
•photos of insects, especially mosquitoes.
•optional: bat headband to wear, plastic bats to add to the decor

Set up
•Place the photos of bats, complete with clothespin, on the A side of the arena.
•Place the photos of flowers and insects on the C side of the arena.
•Have the bat information cards in your pocket or handy.

Skills
•riding: walk on, steering, whoa
•gross/fine motor skills
•listening
•following directions

•counting
•speaking
•communication
•creativity

Introduction to the game
At meet and greet time ask riders if anyone has seen a bat. When is a good time to watch for bats? How should you behave around bats? (Remain calm, and do not touch!) During stretches, fly like a bat. Then wrap your arms around yourself and pretend to sleep, but not upside down!

At game time
Riders gather at the A side of the arena facing the C side. Each rider picks up one of the bat photos and clips it on the horse's mane. The insects and nectar that the bats want are all up at the C end, but to get there riders must answer the questions on the bat cards. Take turns answering questions. Every attempted answer (Volunteers may help.) earns a few steps, number determined by the instructor. Correct answers get an extra step. Encourage guessing. This isn't a quiz, just a way to get talking and thinking. Play until all the bats have reached their food. Suggest that riders can watch for bats at dusk and be thankful that the bats are eating the bugs.

••••••••••••••••

Beautiful Jim Key
Riders learn about a horse who could spell by taking letters from a rack and placing them on another rack. Riders try their hand at matching letters.

Equipment needed
•photos of the horse Beautiful Jim Key http://www.beautifuljimkey.com/
(Be sure and find a photo of Jim with a letter in his mouth.)
•cards with letters that match the letters in the arena -- You may want to add some letters to the dressage letters.
•a mailbox accessible to riders, mounted on the rail or sitting on top of a barrel
•optional: copy of the book Beautiful Jim Key

Set up
•Place the photos of Jim Key in the arena.
•Place the mailbox in the arena.
•Place the letter cards in the mailbox.

Skills
•riding: walk on, whoa, steering, trotting, reverse turn
•letter recognition and matching
•gross/fine motor skills

Introduction to the game

At meet and greet, ask if anyone has ever heard of a horse who could spell and do math. Beautiful Jim Key was such a horse. He lived from 1889 to 1912 and traveled the country for nine years doing shows with his master. He appeared at the World's Fair in St Louis in 1904.

Bill Key, Jim's master, was born a slave in Tennessee in 1833. He was always good with animals and kind with people. After the Civil War, when Bill was a free man, he opened a hospital for horses. He tried to breed the fastest race horse, but the colt, which he named Jim Key, couldn't stand for weeks. The colt was smart and learned to take apples from a drawer and then close the drawer. Bill taught his horse with kindness and patience and claimed that Jim could read, write, spell, do math, tell time and sort the mail. During stretches, riders should count as they stretch up, down, and around. They should sort the mail, and look at their watches, and close the drawer full of apples.

At game time

Riders gather at the mailbox. Each rider takes a letter card from the box and rides (walking or trotting at instructor's discretion) to the corresponding letter in the arena. Come back and do it again until all the letters are gone. Can you spell any words with the letters in the mailbox? Beautiful Jim could spell by taking letters from a rack and putting them on another rack.

. . . .

The World's Smallest Horse?

In this activity riders learn how to measure a horse. It is meant to be done at the beginning of a lesson before riders are mounted.

Equipment needed

•a cardboard "hand" 4" wide
•a strip of cardboard 17.5" tall and about 5 or 6" wide -- This is how tall Thumbelina actually is. On this cardboard write the following information:

> --Thumbelina, the World's Smallest Horse (?)
> --17.5 inches
> --4.1 hands
> --57 pounds
> --eats: one cup of grain, one handful of hay two times per day
> --dwarf mini chestnut mare
> --born May 1, 2001, at 8.5 pounds, 10" tall

•photos of Thumbelina, available on the internet -- Einstein, born in 2010 in New Hampshire, is smaller than Thumbelina as of this writing, but he cannot be entered into the Guinness Book of World Records until he is older.
•a horse measuring stick or tape in hands, if available

Set up

No set up necessary. Hooray!

Skills
•measuring
•listening
•making comparisons
•communication

Introduction to the game
During grooming and tacking, show riders pictures of Thumbelina. Compare the cardboard cutout of Thumbelina's size to the horses being groomed and tacked. Use the cardboard "hand" or the horse measuring tape to measure the horses present. Compare the largest and smallest horses on your farm. Can Thumbelina walk under your horse, or another horse on the farm?

....

Quidditch on Horseback
This game is based on the Harry Potter series. Riders use horses instead of broomsticks to play the game!

Equipment needed:
•one tennis ball to represent the snitch
•one other ball, different from the tennis ball, to represent the quaffle
•two swim "noodles" taped into circles and put on a post -- Hollow, plastic stanchion posts work well. Wrap a Kwiktwist around the noodle making a "handle" at the bottom of the circle, take the ball off the top of the plastic stanchion post, and place the Kwiktwist handle down into the post.
•one magic wand
•one sign: Welcome to Hogwarts Quidditch Arena

Set up
•Place the Hogwarts sign in the arena.
•Place the two noodle goals, one in front of the other, about a foot or two apart in the center of the arena. The hoops should be vertical and parallel to one another, and the same height.
•Hide the tennis ball snitch. Be tricky with this!
•Have the magic wand handy.

Skills
riding: walk on, steering, whoa, trotting if able, standing still
•gross motor skills
•imagination/creativity
•speaking
•taking turns
•competition

Introduction to the game
At meet and greet, ask riders if anyone knows the rules of Quidditch. It is generally played on a flying broomstick, but a horse will work. Usually there are two beaters, three chasers, one keeper and one seeker per team, but today each rider is his or her own team, each representing a different house at Hogwarts. Discuss the game as appropriate. Modified rules to be explained

at game time. During stretches, riders must try and make their broomsticks go up and down and throw the quaffle. Leave the snitch out of it for now.

At game time

Riders meet the instructor near one end of the arena. Riders choose the house they will represent: Gryffindor, Hufflepuff, Ravenclaw, or Slytherin. Riders will take turns trying to make a goal with the quaffle for ten points. At all times riders are now on the lookout for the snitch. Ride to the hoops. The Instructor decides the appropriate distance to the hoops. Stand sideways to the hoops so the quaffle is not thrown over the horse's head. The ball must go through BOTH hoops to score. While the rider is tossing, another rider holds the magic wand and is nearby sending a "spell" to keep the quaffle from going through the hoops. All take turns at tossing the quaffle and casting the spells. At any time during play, if a rider sees the snitch, he or she may ride to the snitch, pick it up (or ask a volunteer for help) and ride to the center of the arena with the snitch in hand, overhead. This is worth twenty-five points (150 in the book, by the way), so the one who finds the snitch may end up being the winner, but others still have a chance. Take turns tossing and casting spells as time and interest allow. Add up the points and see which house won! If riders are capable and the instructor is brave, add trotting to the hoops or trotting to the snitch to make the game more interesting.

Games for September

Capture Your Mountain!
The Great Seal of the United States
Apple Fun
State of Maine Poker Ride
Fall Leaves Tree Hunt

Capture Your Mountain!
This game is a cross between capture the flag and musical stalls.

Equipment needed
•one tall orange traffic cone per rider, open at the top
•one "flag" per rider -- Use a Kwiktwist for the pole of the flag and a bandana for the flag. Making the flags different colors is good.
•music which can start and stop

Set up
•Place the cones equally spaced in a straight line in the center of the arena A to C, with room to go around the outside of them.
•Place the pole of a flag in the top of each cone.
•Have music available to start and stop.

Skills
•riding: walk on, whoa, steering, keeping the proper distance from other horses
•listening
•following directions
•problem solving
•competition
•gross motor skills

Introduction to the game
This game really needs no introduction until game time. No particular stretches necessary.

At game time
Each rider is assigned to a specific cone and rides to it, with all riders facing E. Riders lean over and pick up the flag. Explain that the cones are the mountains, and each rider captures his or her own mountain by placing a flag down through the top of it. Remind riders to be aware that horses in general do not like things waving over their heads, so keep the flags fairly still. When the music starts, riders ride forward to the rail and all turn left. (Everyone must go the same way.) When the music stops, riders proceed as quickly as possible to their own cone and place the flag in the cone. Wait until all have accomplished this. It doesn't matter which direction anyone faces at this time. There is a winner each time, but no one is eliminated. Play again as many times as is appropriate.

The Great Seal of the United States
In this game riders toss stars and complete a representation of part of the seal of the United States.

Equipment needed
•a picture of the Great Seal obverse: http://en.wikipedia.org/wiki/File:US-GreatSeal-Obverse.svg
•a one dollar bill
•thirteen cutout five-pointed stars about five inches across
•one hula hoop

Set up
•Place the hula hoop on the ground in the center of the arena.
•Place the thirteen stars around the arena where riders can reach them.
•Place the photo of the obverse of the Great Seal in the arena for riders to see.
•Have the dollar bill in your pocket.

Skills
•riding: walk on, whoa, steering, standing still
•listening
•gross motor skills

Introduction to the game
At meet and greet, show the riders the picture of the Great Seal of the United States. Tell them the seal was created and adopted in 1782. There is a reverse side, but we are focusing on the obverse side. The seal is used on international treaties.

Ask if anyone knows what "E pluribus unum" means. (One out of many.) Ask if riders know why there are thirteen stripes on the flag of the seal (and on the United States flag). Notice that the eagle, our national symbol, is holding an olive branch representing peace and arrows representing war. He is looking toward the olive branches, meaning peace is stronger than war. During stretches fly like an eagle. Shoot arrows. Make the peace sign. All of you have seen this seal on something very common. Who knows what that is? Show the back of a dollar bill. There you will see both the obverse and the reverse sides.

At game time
Riders meet the instructor in the middle of the arena near the hula hoop. Show the riders the picture of the Great Seal again. The thirteen stars in the cloud above the eagle's head represent the thirteen original colonies. Each rider is to ride to a star, pick it up, return to the hoop and toss the star in. Continue one star at a time until all thirteen stars are in the hoop.

....

Apple Fun
This game is a modified pole bending and apple and spoon, with lots of facts about apples.

Equipment needed
•one apple tree per rider -- Use the same hoops used in Quidditch for trees. (See page 68 for photo.)
•apple cutouts, in red, green, and yellow, each with a fact/question as follows:
> --What can you make with apples?
> --The apple is in the rose family.
> --Washington state produces 60% of U.S. apples.
> --Apples can be stored for months.
> --The apple is an important food grown in all cooler climates.
> --"Johnny Appleseed" (John Chapman) introduced the apple to large parts of Ohio, Indiana, and Illinois.
> --China is the top apple-producing country.

--Insects, usually honey bees, are needed to pollinate apple blossoms.
--The apple tree is probably the earliest tree to have been cultivated.
--All of today's apples come from one species still growing in the NW China/ Kazakhstan border.
--There are more than 7,500 types of apples.
--Who eats apples?
--What color are apples? (red, yellow, green...and white on the inside!)
•cones or posts for an "orchard"
•one large spoon per rider
•one small apple per rider
•optional: different types of apples to show, or even taste.

Set up
•Place two rows of cones parallel to each other to represent an orchard. Add a third row if you have a third rider, and a fourth for the fourth rider. The rows run from A toward C.
•At the C end of each row, place an "apple tree" with apple cutouts on it.
•Have large spoons handy in the arena.

Skills
•riding: walk on, whoa, steering, reverse turn, trotting, riding with one hand
•reading
•communication
•focus

Introduction to the game
At meet and greet, ask how many riders have ever been apple picking. During stretches riders can pick and eat apples, prune the apple trees, climb the trees and bake a pie.

At game time
Riders meet the instructor at the A end of the arena, facing the C end. Each rider faces his or her row of "trees" with the tree with apples at the end. Each rider weaves in and out of his or her particular row of trees and takes one apple from the tree at the end. He or she takes it straight back at the trot if able, and shares the information with the group. Continue until all the apples have been picked.

Riders again face the C end of the arena. Each rider gets one small apple to place on a spoon. Ride straight up to the hoop tree, turn around it, and come back to A.

••••••••••••••

State of Maine Poker Ride
Customize this for your own state, or enjoy a ride through Maine. This is set up for three riders but is easily modified for two or four. Riders collect cards and take a chance on their poker hands.

Equipment needed
•one deck of cards

•a map of Maine with Augusta (A), Bar Harbor (B), "The County" (C) (actually Aroostook County), Fryeburg Fair (F), and Katahdin (K) marked. A simple outline map works, or a roadmap.
•a reference guide to poker hands for each volunteer

> best to worst hands:
> royal flush: 10 thru Ace same suit (unbeatable)
> straight flush: five in a row same suit
> four of a kind
> full house: three of kind and pair
> flush: all same suit
> straight: five in row
> three of a kind
> two pair
> one pair
> high card

•a direction card as follows for each rider to help with "traffic"

> Rider one: start at H, then ride to each letter in order: ABCFK, end at X
> Rider two: start at M, then ride to: CAKBF, end at X
> Rider three: start at X, then ride to FKBAC, end at X

•For this game, it is really helpful to have one volunteer per rider, at least.

Set up
•Shuffle the deck of cards and place ten or eleven cards at each of the letters A,B,C,F,K.
•Give each volunteer a reference guide to poker hands.
•Place the Maine map in the arena.

Skills
•riding: walk on, steering, whoa, standing still, keeping proper distance from other horses, reverse turn
•problem solving
•gross motor skills
•communication
•competition

Introduction to the game
At meet and greet, mention that the arena represents the state of Maine today. A is the capital, Augusta, B is for Bar Harbor, C is for "the County" or Aroostook, F is for Fryeburg Fair, and K is for Katahdin, the highest mountain in the state. Can anyone think of place names in Maine for the rest of the letters in the arena? (Minot, Hebron, Eastport...) During stretches, do things you can do in Maine: swim, ski, hike, bike, pick apples, kayak, snow shoe, rock climb, etc.

At game time
Rider one rides to the letter H. Rider two rides to the letter M, and rider three rides to the letter X (center of arena). Each rider receives the direction card and proceeds to the first letter. Here the volunteer picks up the cards, spreads them, and allows the rider to choose a card. The rider must reach up, or over, or low. The rider should show the volunteer the card but not any other riders. The volunteer replaces the remaining cards. Continue on to each letter. Each rider goes to the center of the arena when all five Maine places have been visited and all five cards collected. Volunteers give the remaining cards to the instructor. Volunteers and riders consult

concerning the poker hand. Each rider may turn in one, two, or three cards to the instructor and receive that many back. Then hands are revealed to determine who has the best hand. (No betting!) The winner leads the "victory" lap, but all participate.

•••••••••••••••

Fall Leaves Tree Hunt

This activity involves matching samples of leaves with trees outside.

Equipment needed

This game can be as complicated or simple as you wish. It is best to do this activity on the trail, but it can be done inside, also.

•A collection of real leaves from different kinds of trees in your area, or photos. I put the leaves on cardboard and cover with clear contact paper. Or have enough leaves of each species to give one to each rider.

Set up

None. Go outside and look for trees.

Skills

•walk on, trail riding, steering, whoa
•observing
•listening

Introduction to the game

At meet and greet, tell riders they are going on a tree hunt. Ask riders if they know why leaves turn colors in the fall. All the colors are in the leaves all summer, but chlorophyll, which makes the leaf green, wins out over all the other colors. In the fall, when the days are still warm but the nights are cool, chlorophyll production slows down and then stops, so the other colors can now appear.

During stretches, riders can pretend to be trees in the wind, leaves falling, or particular trees: the mighty oak, the weeping willow, the giant sequoia, etc.

At game time (on the trail)

Give riders one, two, three or more types of leaves to feel and identify. Modify as necessary according to the rider. While on the trail, look for the leaves. Have any trees changed color yet? What trees don't lose their leaves? How are those leaves (needles) different from the other leaves? Enjoy being out on a fall day! What do you smell? Do different leaves have different smells? At the end of your ride, put your leaves (if they are not in plastic) in a compost pile, or take them home.

Games for October

The Great Wall of China

In this game the arena becomes the Great Wall, and riders ride along it collecting photos and facts.

Equipment needed
•a set of six pictures of the Great Wall of China from the internet
•a Great Wall of China map
•six envelopes, each with a question on the outside and a photo on the inside. The answer to the question goes on the back of the picture.

> --How long do you think the Great Wall of China is? The Great Wall is not built in a single line, but in many connected sections. It is around 4,000 miles long.
> --How old do you think the Great Wall of China is? The Great Wall was built by hand over hundreds of years beginning perhaps as early as 700 BCE.
> --What is the Great Wall made of? It is made of bricks, rocks, and packed earth.
> --How wide is the Great Wall? It is generally about 15 feet wide, paved in bricks set in lime. Horsemen could ride over many parts of the wall.
> --Can the Great Wall be seen from the moon? No, but it can be seen from earth's orbit.
> --What is the Chinese name for the Great Wall? In Chinese the Great Wall is called Wan-Li Qang-Qeng, which means 10,000 Li Wall. One Li is equal to 5,000 kilometers. (The Q is pronounced "ch".)

•Six signs for the arena, names of places along the wall:
(from west to east)

> Jiaya Pass
> Bedaling (the most popular tourist spot on the Wall)
> Mutianyu
> Jinshanling
> Simatia (popular because of the zip line from the top of the Wall to the valley below)
> Tiger Mountain

Set up
•Place the name cards around the arena.
•Place an envelope at each name card.
•Place a map of the Wall at Jiaya Pass, where the game will start.

Skills
•riding: walk on, steering, whoa, riding side by side while keeping proper distance
•creativity
•speaking
•reading
•taking turns

Introduction to the game
At meet and greet, ask who has heard of the Great Wall of China. Ask riders to share information they might know about it. During stretches, riders should be looking for the enemy from the wall, crouching down behind the horse's neck to hide from the enemy, eating with chopsticks, and playing pingpong.

At game time

Riders meet at Jiaya Pass to start their trip along the wall. Riders should ride together side by side, keeping enough space for safety, instead of one behind the other. Have a volunteer remove the envelope from the rail and ask the question. Riders think up answers. Riders take turns opening the envelope to find the picture and the answer. Move to the next place along the Wall and continue in the same manner until you have reached Tiger Mountain, several thousand miles from Jiaya Pass!

. . . .

Columbus Day Voyage

This game is about getting from Spain to the New World on horseback, an interesting feat.

Equipment needed

•a map of Spain or a sign that says "Spain"
•a map of Hispaniola or a sign that says "The New World"
•sign that says "The Atlantic Ocean"
•optional: a world map showing Columbus's route
•a set of game cards which determine how far each rider goes as follows:

    -- Smooth sailing. Move ahead five steps walking.
    -- Albatross falls on deck. Take two steps backwards.
    -- Sailors all very happy. Trot ahead six steps.
    -- Compass broken. Turn around and take two steps. Turn around again.
    -- Man overboard. Take two steps backwards.
    -- Full moon, rising tide. Trot ahead six steps.
    -- High seas. Move only two steps walking.
    -- Captain fell asleep at the wheel. Lose one turn.
    -- Good sailing. Move ahead four steps walking.
    -- Good weather. Move ahead four steps walking.
    -- Sun comes out after days of rain. Winds come up. Walk ahead ten steps.
    -- Good sailing weather. Move ahead six steps walking
    -- Everyone is seasick. Walk ahead four steps very slowly.
    -- Sailors are arguing. Walk ahead only two steps.
    -- Sailors frightened. Go back to Spain.
    -- Fantastic winds. Trot directly to the New World.
    -- Warm breezes. Everyone very happy. Trot ahead six steps.
    -- Sailors spy land! Trot ahead six steps.

Set up

Place the map of Spain at the letter A. Place the New World at the letter K. Place the Atlantic Ocean sign somewhere along the rail, perhaps near B. Have the cards handy and shuffled.

Skills

•riding: walk on, trotting, whoa, reverse turn, keeping proper distance from other horses
•counting
•taking turns
•competition

Introduction to the game

Ask if anyone knows why school is closed on the second Monday of October. Some people consider Columbus Day a controversial holiday; however, Columbus did land somewhere in the New World on October 12, 1492. In this game, we simply "sail" from Spain to the New World. During stretches, get out the spy glasses and look for land, hoist the sails, swab the deck, and steer the ship's wheel.

At game time

Riders meet at Spain. Riders take turns taking a card and following the directions. Modify cards as necessary! First one to arrive in the New World has to wait for the others to arrive.

••••••••••••••••

Pumpkin Decorating

In this activity, riders collect parts of a face and place them on a pumpkin.

Equipment needed
•large cardboard or poster board pumpkin, or a large, real pumpkin
•black eyes, nose, mouth
•optional: Make several different types of eyes, noses, and mouths. Make ears or other things to decorate the pumpkin with.

Set up
•Place the large cardboard pumpkin in the arena where riders can reach it. Or place the real pumpkin on a barrel in the center of the arena.
•Place the eyes, nose, mouth and any other parts near the pumpkin on a barrel.

Skills
•riding: walk on, whoa, steering, standing still
•gross/fine motor skills
•taking turns
•speaking

Introduction to the game

At meet and greet, ask who has carved a pumpkin for Halloween. During stretches clean out the pumpkin and carve the face. Eat pumpkin pie.

At game time

Riders take turns choosing face parts, naming them, and putting them on the pumpkin. Admire each work of art before the next rider has a turn. Or alternate one rider putting an eye and another putting the mouth, etc.

The Great Pumpkin Roundup

This is actually three games involving pumpkins: trivia, pumpkin and spoon, and "pumpkin" toss.

Equipment needed:

•two posts per rider, one with a foam swimming "noodle" bent and duck taped into a circle (This is the same hoop used for Quidditch. See photo on page 68.)
•one bucket per rider plus one
•one orange bean bag per rider
•one orange "pumpkin cup" per rider placed upside down over a post
•one mini pumpkin per rider
•one large spoon per rider
•optional: pumpkin seeds for prizes
•one set of pumpkin trivia cards as follows: (one fact per card)

> --Are pumpkins good for you? Why or why not? Yes, they are low in fat and calories and have lots of vitamin A and C and potassium
> --What percent of a pumpkin is water? 90%
> --Besides eating them, what else did native Americans do with pumpkins? cut them into strips, flattened them, dried them, and made mats
> --Where were pumpkins first grown and when? Mexico, more than 7,000 years ago
> --Where are pumpkins grown? all over the world except Antarctica
> --At latest count, how big was the largest pumpkin? one ton at this writing
> --What colors do pumpkins come in? orange, white, blue (Australia), green (unripe), and tan (commercial)
> --Are pumpkins a fruit or a vegetable? fruit (grows from a flower)
> --What state grows the most pumpkins? Illinois, nearly 500 million pounds
> --Why do we carve pumpkins on Halloween? old Celtic tradition, to welcome home the spirits of ancestors, to ward off evil spirits, to keep the restless soul "Stingy Jack" away. The Irish brought the tradition of carving turnips to the U. S.
> --How do you fix a broken pumpkin? with a pumpkin patch

Set up

•Place one post for each rider at one end of the arena. (near A)
•On top of these posts place an orange bean bag, and upside down over that, an orange plastic cup (if available).
•Opposite these posts at the other end of the arena (near C) place the posts with foam hoops attached.
•Place a bucket behind each hoop.
•Place the extra bucket with the spoons and mini pumpkins near A for easy access.
•Have pumpkin trivia cards in your pocket.

Skills

•riding skills: walk on, steering, whoa, standing still, backing up, riding with one hand
•problem solving
•gross and fine motor skills
•following directions
•creativity
•counting
•competition

•taking turns

Introduction to the Game
Obviously this game is great for just before Halloween. The week before you are going to play it, invite riders to come in costumes which are SAFE, will not scare the horses, and can be ridden in comfortably. Masks and costumes which make noise are not allowed. I invite volunteers to come in costume also. I wear some simple costume which will not interfere with teaching or scare the horses, such as The Great Pumpkin tee shirt. During meet and greet, welcome riders to the great pumpkin roundup. Ask who has carved a pumpkin, who likes pumpkins, who grows pumpkins, etc.

Stretching ideas: be a fat pumpkin, be a tall pumpkin, be a slumpy pumpkin, pick pumpkins, throw pumpkins, be the winner of growing the biggest pumpkin, and pretend there is a pumpkin on your head.

At game time: three games in the roundup!
Riders line up at the C end of arena facing A, where the posts with cups are placed.

Pumpkin Trivia: Riders must answer a trivia question about pumpkins. Move 4 steps forward if the answer is correct, 3 if it is incorrect. Riders are encouraged to make up an answer, with help from volunteers if necessary. Crazy answers encouraged and enjoyed! The object is to get to the orange cups at the other end of the arena. Modify the number of steps and the difficulty of the questions as necessary.

Pumpkin Toss: Riders are now at the A end of the arena. They should turn around to face the C end and stand behind the post with orange cups. At "go", riders pick up the cup and bean bag. Place the bean bag in the cup and carry it to the hoop at the other end. Toss the bean bag from the cup through the hoop aiming for the bucket. Give as many tries as necessary. Once the bag is in the bucket, toss the cup in after it. Ride around the hoop keeping right and ride back to the post near A.

Pumpkin and Spoon: Riders are at their posts facing the hoops. Each rider receives a large spoon with a mini pumpkin placed on it. Ride to the hoop, go around it keeping right; ride back to the post. Trotting may of course be added with more able riders who want a challenge! Pumpkins may be tossed into the bucket that is at A.

. . . .

How do you spell HORSE?
This is a game of matching letters with the nautical symbols for letters, inspired by a set of nautical flags.

Equipment needed
•Ideally, a set of nautical flags. I just happened to have a set in the basement, which is why I developed this game. But go to http://www.soundkeepers.com/kids/alphabet/ and you'll be able to print out each letter. Click on the letter to get a large, clear version of the flag with the letter. Print two copies of the letters H, O, R, S, E .

•Cut out the flag portion for one H, O, R, S, and E from the above printouts, so now you have one printout with the letter H and the flag, and one of the flag separately. If you have a set of nautical flags (rather doubtful, I know), you can skip that last step.
•Look up the flag and meaning for each rider's first initial. Print out the flag for the rider's first initial (G for Greg).

Set up
•Place the printouts with the letters and flags, one each for H, O, R, S, and E, around the arena where the riders can reach them, mixed up.
•Place the flags for H, O, R, S, and E around the arena, also in mixed order.
•Put each rider's initial/flag printout in the arena.

Skills
•riding: walk on, steering, whoa
•reading
•sequencing
•problem solving
•gross motor skills

Introduction to the game
At meet and greet, ask riders if anyone has ever seen nautical flags. Explain that they are used between ships at sea or ship and shore, and were first invented in 1855. The colors used are particularly visible at sea: red, blue, yellow, black, and white. Each letter also has a meaning attached to it. During stretches riders should pull up the anchor, use the tiller to steer the boat, put up the sail, look for pirates, point to a whale.

At game time
Riders gather in the center of the arena. Each rider must find one letter and the flag that matches it. Continue finding the letters and flags until all are gathered. Each rider then finds his or her initial and picks it up. Return to the center of the arena. Spell out the word horse with the flags. Each rider says what his initial means as a flag. For example, the flag for "H" means "I have a pilot on board."

Games for November

Election Day!

In this game riders get to vote for their favorite horse.

Equipment needed
•a ballot per rider with horses of your farm listed
•a ballot box with a slot in the top
•a barrel
•pencils
•a "stop box" made with four poles on the ground

Set up
•Place the stop box with four poles on the ground in the arena.
•Place the barrel with the ballot box on top next to the "stop box".
•Place the pencils and the ballots on the barrel.

Skills
•riding: walk on, steering, whoa, standing still
•communication (name and address or town)
•fine motor skills

Introduction to the game
At meet and greet, ask riders if they know when Election Day is and why. Ask riders if they know what Election Day is. Election Day was set in 1845 and is the first Tuesday after the first Monday of November. When it was established, people had to travel to the county seat to vote. No one could travel on a Sunday because of church. November 1st is All Saints' Day (considered a Holy Day of obligation in some faiths), so that wouldn't work. Also merchants used to do their books on the first of each month and couldn't travel. November was chosen because the harvest would be in, but the weather would still be mild. Ask riders why it is important to vote.

During stretches riders should pretend they are candidates and wave, shake hands, make the V symbol for victory, and bow.

At game time
Riders meet the instructor in the center of the arena. To vote in an election in the U.S., one must be a citizen and at least eighteen years old. For this game, all can vote. Women could not vote in all states until 1920. Today, one at a time, each rider will ride to the "polls" (the stop box), stop, say his or her name and address (or town, as able). Then each will vote for his or her favorite horse. If it is a presidential election year, ask who can run for president. (Natural born U.S. citizen, thirty-five years old or more, resident of the U. S. at least fourteen years.) Riders can count ballots at the end of the lesson and celebrate the favorite horse, or horses.

In Honor of Veterans Day

This simple card-making activity helps riders remember those who have served our country in the military. It builds good relations and teaches the riders to thank others for making sacrifices.

Equipment needed
•one small clipboard per rider
•one pencil, pen, or marker per rider
•one thank you card per rider (or blank card)
•optional: patriotic stickers
•a list of the veterans associated with your establishment

Set up
There is really no set up for this activity. Just have the above list of items in the arena, perhaps on a barrel.

Skills
riding: whoa, standing still
•communication
•small motor skills
•creativity

Introduction to the game
At meet and greet, ask why there is no school on November 11. Veterans Day honors all those who have served in the military, in war or in peace, and is November 11. The armistice to end the fighting of "The Great War" (WWI) occurred on November 11 at 11 a.m., 1918. The first holiday was in 1919 and was called Armistice Day by then President Wilson. In 1938 it became a Federal holiday, and in 1954 President Eisenhower had Congress change the name to Veterans Day. The five branches of the military are Army, Navy, Marine Corps, Air Force, and Coast Guard. Ask riders who knows a veteran. Share the list of veterans associated with your farm. Tell riders today's activity involves thanking our veterans. During stretches, riders may practice saluting, signing an armistice, sitting very tall, and waving.

At game time
Riders meet the instructor at the barrel. The instructor passes out clip boards, markers, stickers, and cards. Riders are asked to draw or write a thank you message to the veterans at your farm. They sign their names or initials, or make a mark. Volunteers are encouraged to help. At the end of all of your lessons, you should have at least one card for each veteran who is associated with your farm. I have found that the veterans really appreciate this simple act of kindness, with no politics involved. Thank the riders for making a good effort.

••••••••••••••

The Turkey Trot!
This game involves putting the feathers on a large turkey while learning some facts about turkeys.

Equipment needed:
•one large cardboard turkey, often available at party stores, covered with contact paper
•one set of nine paper "feathers", laminated, which can be placed on the cardboard turkey, with facts on the back of each one as follows:

--Native Americans used turkey feathers on their arrows and their ceremonial clothing.
--Wild turkeys spend the night in trees. They especially like oak trees.
--45 million turkeys are eaten each Thanksgiving.
--Male turkeys (toms) gobble. Females (hens) do not.
--Wild turkeys can run up to 20 miles per hour.
--Turkeys can see movement up to 100 yards away.
--Ben Franklin thought the turkey should be our national bird.
--Turkeys lived almost 10 million years ago.
-- Turkey eggs take 28 days to hatch.

Set up
•Place the large turkey in the arena where riders can reach it.
•Place the turkey "feathers" all around the arena where riders can reach them.

Skills
•riding: walk on, whoa, steering, trotting
•gross/fine motor skills
•reading
•speaking

Introduction to the game
At meet and greet, ask who has seen a wild turkey. Ask the riders who eats turkey at Thanksgiving. Tell the riders that they will learn some facts about turkeys during the game. During stretches riders can fly, flap wings, move necks like a walking turkey, eat turkey, pluck a turkey, stuff a turkey, bake a turkey.

At game time
Riders meet the instructor at the cardboard turkey. Riders are then sent out to find feathers for the turkey. Riders can bring back only one feather at a time. Read the back, with help if necessary. This is not a race. If able, riders may trot the feather back to the turkey, place it on the bird, and walk back for another feather. Continue until all feathers are on the bird. Gather back at the cardboard turkey. Each rider shares one thing learned from the back of the feathers.

....

Over the River and Through the Woods
In this game, based on the familiar song, riders must work their way to Grandmother's house by following directions.

Equipment needed
•a bucket with "snow" (plastic snow flakes, or Ivory Snow flakes, or your own idea)
•a bucket with jars of "bubbles"
•a couple of signs with arrows which say "GRANDMOTHER'S HOUSE"

•a sign/drawing which says "Grandmother's House,"
• A sign which says, "We are thankful for..." on a poster board with a pad of super sticky post-it notes stuck to it.
•several markers or pens
•two ground poles to make the river/bridge
•posts topped with green cones to make the woods
•five large file cards with a number on one side and part of the song written as follows:
•optional: a copy of <u>Over the River and Through the Wood</u>, A Thanksgiving Poem by Lydia Maria Child illustrated with woodcuts by Christopher Manson

-- Card 1
Over the river and through the woods
To Grandmother's house we go.
(Go over the river and through the woods.)

-- Card 2
The horse knows the way to carry the sleigh
Through the white and drifted snow.
(Find the snow. Follow the arrows. Touch the snow.)

-- Card 3
Over the river and through the woods
Trot fast my dapple gray!
(Go back and trot over the river and through the woods.)

-- Card 4
Hoorah for the fun!
Is the pudding done?
(Ride to the bucket of bubbles and have fun!)

-- Card 5
Hoorah for Thanksgiving Day!
(Ride to Grandmother's house and whoa.)

Set up
•Place 2 ground poles parallel to one another to represent a bridge over the river.
•Set up the posts with green cones as the forest for the riders to wind through on the other side of the river.
•Beyond the forest place a bucket of "snow" on the ground or on a barrel.
•Put up some arrows for directions.
•Beyond the snow, place the bucket with the bubbles.
•Beyond the bubbles is Grandmother's House.
•Place the five file cards with the poem/song along the rail at logical places. Use your imagination and set this up in whatever way works best for you and your arena.

Skills
•riding: walk on, trotting, steering, whoa, standing still, keeping proper distance from other horses
•following directions
•reading
•listening
•singing
•communication
•fine motor skills

Introduction to the game
At meet and greet, sing together "Over the River and Through the Woods" and talk about Thanksgiving. Ask riders to be thinking about what they are thankful for. For stretches, make arms move in rhythmic, horizontal fashion to show waves in "over the river." For "through the woods" have riders push branches away from their faces. For "Grandmother's House" draw a house in the air. Use hands/arms to make snow coming down. "Eat" dinner! Other stretches might involve throwing a football, carving a turkey, rubbing one's stomach.

At game time

Riders meet at card number 1, read it and follow the directions, riding to card number 2. Continue in this way until riders arrive at Grandmother's House. Tell each rider what you are thankful for, and ask each one to tell you. Those who are able can write it on one of the sticky notes and put it on the poster. Others can dictate to volunteers. Volunteers should join in. By the end of the week before Thanksgiving, the poster should be filled with what we are all thankful for.

• • • • • • • • • • • • •

Santa's Reindeer
Riders must work their way toward Santa's reindeer by answering questions about reindeer.

Equipment needed
•one set of antlers per rider, made by using two Kwiktwists
•one post for each set of antlers -- Put each Kwitwist antler in the top of a post.
•several photos of reindeer, including one close up of their hooves
•two plastic rings per rider.
•one set of reindeer fact cards as follows:
  --Santa's reindeer are: Dasher, Dancer, Prancer,
  Vixen, Comet, Cupid, Donner, Blitzen, and on foggy nights,
  Rudolf.

--What does a reindeer eat? Reindeer eat grass in summer and reindeer moss (lichen) in winter

--Who has antlers? Both males and females have antlers.

--What are reindeer used for, aside from pulling Santa's sleigh? Reindeer have been domesticated for centuries and can pull sleds or be used as pack animals. They are used for milk and meat, and their skin and fur are used to make tents, boots, and clothing.

--Where do reindeer live? Reindeer live throughout the Arctic region, and of course with Santa.

--What's special about a reindeer's nose? Reindeer have a special nose which warms cold air before it enters the lungs. The nose stays moist from the outgoing air. Reindeer have a keen sense of smell.

--What keeps a reindeer warm? Reindeer have a double coat to keep them warm, with a woolly undercoat and a long-haired overcoat of hollow fibers to trap the air.

--Does a reindeer chew a cud like a cow? Yes, a reindeer is a ruminant with four sections of stomach, and it chews a cud.

--What is a reindeer's hoof like? Each reindeer hoof has four "toes," two large in front and two smaller behind. The bottoms of the feet are spongey in summer on the wet tundra and sharp-rimmed in the winter for traction on the snow and ice and for digging.

Set up
•Place the "antlers" along the C side of the arena.
•Place the rings on the A side of the arena where you can easily reach them.
•Place the photos of reindeer around the arena.
•Have the reindeer fact cards in your pocket.

Skills
•riding: walk on, steering, whoa, standing still
•communication
•taking turns
•small motor skills
•counting
•reading

Introduction to the game
At meet and greet, ask the riders who can name Santa's reindeer. See if as a group you can name them. Hand the card with the names to a rider who can read, or a volunteer, and check to see if you were right. Ask how a reindeer is like a horse, (both mammals, for starters), and how they are different. (Horses can't fly!) During stretches riders can dig for moss, toss their heads, fly.

At game time
Riders line up on the A side of the arena facing the C side and the "antlers." Riders will earn their way up the arena by trying to answer the reindeer questions. Volunteers may help. Making an attempt gets you on your way, right or wrong. Take turns asking riders the questions and having them advance a certain number of steps, determined by your arena set up. When riders arrive at the antlers, hand them two rings each and ask them to place the rings on the antlers. Return to A, and see who can remember one fact about reindeer.

Games for December

Saint Nicholas Day, December 6

In this game riders learn about Saint Nicholas and try their hand at tossing coins into a boot.

Equipment needed
•one large, winter boot
•"gold" coins
•a barrel
•one hoop on a post (See page 68 for a photo.)
•one set of file cards, laminated, as follows:

   --front side: ST -- back: I was born in what is now Turkey in the 3rd Century.

   --front side: NI -- back: My wealthy parents died in an epidemic and I devoted my life to helping others.

   --front side: CH -- back: I became the Bishop of Myra. I helped children, sailors, and people in need.

   --front side: OL -- back: Once I helped a poor man who had three daughters who would have been sold into slavery because they had no money. I tossed three gold coins through an open window and they landed in a boot.

   --front side: AS -- back: I died on December 6, 343. December 6 is now my special day, and there are many countries that celebrate my day. Can you toss the coins through the "window" into the boot?

Set up
•Place the five laminated cards around the arena out of order.
•Place the boot on the barrel in the arena, and have the coins handy.
•Place the hoop on a post in front of the boot. This represents the window in the story.

Skills
•riding: walk on, steering, whoa, standing still
•sequencing
•reading/communication
•gross motor skills

Introduction to the game
At meet and greet, ask if anyone has ever heard of St. Nicholas. Ask if anyone knows that he was a real person who lived a very long time ago. Explain that in some countries there is a special day for St. Nicholas, and in France it is traditional to give candy on that day. In some countries St. Nicholas Day is the day gifts are given, not Christmas. During stretches reach as high as you can. Pretend there is candy in the sky for you to grab! When you reach it, share it with others.

At game time
Riders meet the instructor in the center of the arena. Point out the cards with letters around the arena. Send riders out to gather the cards, one card per rider. Send riders back as necessary to get the rest of the cards. All return to the center of the arena. Look at all the cards and see if anyone can figure out what they spell. Volunteers may help. Once St. Nicholas is spelled out, have riders or volunteers read the backs. Next riders take turns seeing how many coins they can throw through the hoop and into the boot. At the end of the lesson, remind riders that St. Nicholas was always trying to help people.

Candy Canes

This game involves decorating a Christmas tree and explores the connection between candy canes and sheep.

Equipment needed
•eight posts with cones on top
•eight cardboard sheep with a pipe cleaner loop on top
•one shepherd's crook per rider, made from a Kwiktwist
•one small, artificial Christmas tree. We have the trunk of ours placed down inside the top of the post.
•optional: one candy cane per rider

Set up
•Place the eight posts with cones in the arena in the shape of a shepherd's crook.
•Place a sheep on each of the cones. Use a small piece of looped masking tape to put the sheep horizontally on the top of the cone, leaving the pipe cleaner hoop free and accessible.
•Place the shepherd's crooks in the arena.
•Place the Christmas tree in the arena, away from the shepherd's crooks.
•optional: place one candy cane per rider on the tree.
(Be sure to use the cones for steering practice during the lesson.)

Skills
•riding: walk on, steering, whoa, standing still
•gross and fine motor skills
•listening
•following directions
•taking turns

Introduction to the game
At meet and greet, ask if anyone knows how or when candy canes were invented, or how they are associated with sheep. A shepherd uses a crook to help keep track of his sheep. It can also be used as a walking stick. A Pharaoh in ancient Egypt carried a crook because it was associated with the Egyptian god Osiris. Christmas pageants have been popular for centuries. A choirmaster in the 1670s had a lively bunch of young boys as shepherds one year. He took the traditional white stick of peppermint candy and bent it to look like a shepherd's crook. He gave the boys the candy to keep them quiet during the pageant, and before long candy canes became popular. The red stripes appeared around 1900, but no one knows exactly when or why.

During stretches, be sure to keep track of your sheep. Lick your candy cane, and remember to do all your stretches so you can stay limber and run after your sheep.

At game time

Riders gather at the bottom of the "candy cane." Each rider steers through the cones, weaving in and out. The second time through the cones, each rider takes a "crook" and tries to capture a sheep. He or she then takes the sheep to the Christmas tree and hangs the sheep on the tree. Continue until all the sheep are on the Christmas tree. If there are real candy canes on the tree, each rider gets one!

••••••••••••••

Decorating the Christmas Tree

Riders will learn about the tradition of the Christmas tree and then decorate one.

Equipment needed
•one artificial Christmas tree
•unbreakable Christmas tree decorations, or various beanie babies

Set up
•Place the Christmas tree in the center of the arena.
•Place the ornaments, or beanie babies, or both, along the rails within reach.

Skills
•riding: walk on, steering, whoa, standing still
•gross motor skills, fine motor skills
•problem solving

Introduction to the game
At meet and greet, ask riders who has a Christmas tree. Ask riders why they do this. The custom of Christmas trees came to the U. S. from Germany and became popular about 100 years ago, but even Romans decorated their houses with evergreens at the time of the winter solstice. Evergreens represent hope for spring and life after death, because they remain green through the winter. During stretches, cut down a tree, drag it home, set it up, decorate it, and lean back in amazement at its beauty.

At game time
Riders meet the instructor in the center of the arena at the Christmas tree. The instructor sends the riders to pick up one ornament at a time and return to the tree to place it on the tree. Continue until the tree is gorgeous and impressive. Sing your favorite Christmas song around the tree.

••••••••••••••

What Santa Needs Race

In this game riders collect and carry items Santa needs on Christmas Eve.

Equipment needed
•a set of large cards with pictures and words as follows:
(Or use the actual items, which is a lot more fun.)

> --a map
> --warm gloves
> --a bell
> --warm socks
> --a warm hat
> --long underwear
> --presents
> --a bag for toys

•a stopwatch or watch with a second hand

Set up
•Place the cards around the arena in no particular order in places where the riders can reach them easily.
•Alternately, place the actual items around the arena so that they are easily collected.
•Have the stopwatch handy.

Skills
•riding: walk on, steering, whoa, trotting
•problem solving
•gross/fine motor skills
•taking turns

Introduction to the game
At meet and greet, ask riders what Santa might need on Christmas Eve, aside from his sleigh and reindeer. During stretches, riders should wiggle their antlers, slide down the chimney with hands over their heads, put presents under the tree, go up the chimney with a finger beside the nose, drive the reindeer, and wave.

At game time
The riders meet the instructor at A. Riders will go one at a time, when the instructor says, "go", and collect the eight items (or cards representing the items) in any order, then return to A at the trot if able, or at a fast walk. The instructor times the rider. A volunteer replaces the items to the same places after each rider. Riders must figure out the quickest way to go. If the actual items are used, talk about picking up the bag first, or let the riders figure out the most efficient way to collect and carry the items.

••••••••••••••

Helping Santa Deliver the Toys
This is an untimed obstacle course with a Santa theme.

Equipment needed
•one sign saying "North Pole" attached to a post
•one drawing of the roof of a house, attached to a post
•one artificial Christmas tree on a post
•one picture of a sleigh per rider, attached to a post, (only one post for all sleighs)
•one picture of Santa's bag per rider, attached to a post (only one post for all bags)
•two ground poles representing the chimney

(The pictures of the sleighs and bags may have clothespins on them, which can then be clipped to the horse's mane. Looped tape on the back also works for sticking the pictures on the horse.)
•optional: an ornament to be given to each rider, perhaps made with his or her picture on the horse

Set up
This can all be set up on an "inner circle" in the arena, thus leaving the area by the rail free for the rest of the lesson.
•Place the North Pole near F
•Place the post with the sleighs near M.
•Place the post with the bags near H.
•Place the post with the rooftop near E.
•Place the Christmas tree on a post near K.
•Place the ground poles parallel to one another aimed at the tree.
•If you have ornaments for the riders, place them on the Christmas tree.

Skills
•riding: walk on, steering, whoa, keeping proper distance from other horses
•following directions
•sequencing
•gross motor skills

Introduction to the game
At meet and greet, tell riders they will be helping Santa deliver the presents today. Ask riders what they are hoping for this year. During stretches, riders should harness the reindeer, drive the sleigh, slide down the chimney, and take the presents out of the bag.

At game time
Riders meet at the North Pole and proceed around the obstacle course, one behind the other, but leaving enough room between riders to avoid collisions. This is not a race. Each rider leaves the North Pole and picks up a sleigh, then picks up a bag of toys. Ride to the rooftop and whoa. Then walk slowly between the ground poles (the chimney) and place the bag of toys on the Christmas tree. Then get out of the way for the next rider! If there are ornaments on the tree for the riders, give them out at this time.

••••••••••••••••

What is Hanukkah?
In this game riders learn the origin and meaning of Hanukkah.

Equipment needed
•one flat menorah made from construction paper and laminated
•nine paper laminated candles, appropriate size for the menorah, numbered on one side and with information on the back as follows:

1: I am the Shamash, or attendant candle. I light the other candles and go in the middle.
2: Hanukkah is an eight-day festival of light.
3: Hanukkah means light wins over darkness.

4: Twenty-one hundred years ago, the Holy Land was ruled by the Greeks.
5: The Greeks wanted to destroy the Jewish religion.
6: The Maccabees, a small group of Jewish soldiers, successfully drove the Greeks away.
7: The Jewish people took back their temple.
8: The people wanted to rededicate their temple by burning an oil lamp but had oil for only one day.
9: The lamp burned for eight days!

Set up
•Place the menorah in the arena where it can be reached.
•Place the candles, number side out, randomly around the arena, where riders can reach them.

Skills
•riding: walk on, steering, whoa, standing still
•reading
•communication
•gross motor skills

Introduction to the game
At meet and greet, ask if anyone knows about or celebrates Hanukkah. If someone in the group celebrates Hanukkah, allow that person to tell the group a bit about it. Tell riders that at game time, they will light the menorah and learn about Hanukkah. During stretches riders should light candles, make latkes, roll the dreidel.

At game time
Riders meet the instructor at the menorah. Explain that Hanukkah is an important holiday in the Jewish faith. The menorah holds the candles, and the holiday lasts for eight days because of the story that they will soon hear. The candles in the arena all have numbers, but only for our

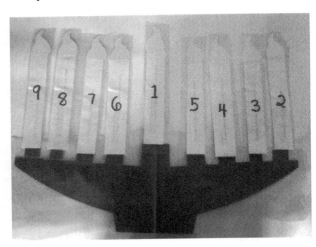

purposes in the arena. The candles are placed in the following manner as you face the menorah: number one goes in the center. Two goes in the far right, and three goes to the left of number two. If one were really lighting a menorah, the candles go into the holder in that order, but the Shamash (number one candle) is used to light the candles, and the candles are lit from left to right. For example, candle number four goes to the left of candle number three, which is to the left of number two. On the third day, the Shamash is lit, then it is used to light number four, then three, then two. This may be too complicated for many riders to understand, and should not overshadow the true meaning of the holiday.

Send the riders out to pick up the candles one at a time in numerical order. Bring each candle back to the menorah, read the back, and place it in the appropriate place on the menorah. Continue until the menorah is full and all candles are "lit."

Other Game Ideas (All have been tested!)

Horse Colors
Because there are so many variations of horse colors, it is simplest to start with the colors of your own herd and build from there. Stick to the basics of chestnut, bay, palomino, gray, black, pinto, brown. Print pictures of horses of each color and have cards with the names of the colors. Have riders choose a card and ride to the appropriate color horse.

Horse Breeds
Get a calendar of horse breeds. Laminate the large photos and label on the back. Give riders facts about each breed. Have riders ride to the Belgian, or the Arab, or the Morgan, etc.

Calendar Match Up
Take any horse calendar and laminate the large photos. Cut the small photos from the back and laminate them also. Have riders choose a small photo and ride to the matching large photo.

Indoor Trail Ride
For a cold winter day when everyone wants to go outside but can't, set the arena up as a trail. Put out a barrel with woodland beanie babies on it. Begin your ride by looking for wildlife. Continue through a "forest" of cones, weaving in and out. Cross over some ground poles where it's muddy and full of flies. Come to a field down the long side where you trot. Ride between two ground poles over the raging river. Take a sharp left and go up the middle of the arena where some poles are lying around. You have to get over the blow down. Then head back over the muddy place, through the forest of cones, and you are back to your barrel. Make up your own scenario, and fill in the sights and sounds!

Stop and Go, for 2, 3, or 4 riders
Riders line up on the A side of the arena facing the C side, each rider near a cone on a post. In the center of the arena between B and E are ground poles, one per rider, parallel to sides C and A. At the far side of the arena are posts with cones on top, and a plastic ring on top of the cone, one per rider. Riders begin at A, ride to the ground pole and whoa with the front legs in front of the pole and the rear legs behind the pole. At the C end of the arena, riders keep right to their post, pick up a ring, and ride back to their starting post, putting the ring on the starting post.

Anything and Spoon
On a hot summer day ice cube and spoon is a lot of fun. Toss the ice cube into a bucket at the end of the game or through a hoop and let it melt on the ground. Potato and spoon works well if you're cooking something up for Thanksgiving. Make a ghoulish dish for Halloween, carrying each ingredient on the spoon and taking it to the cauldron. (grape eyeballs, spaghetti intestines, gummi worms, etc.)

Treasure Hunts
These are always fun, but they require advance planning and orchestration. I have used different colored file cards to keep everyone straight and have included instructions about speed as well as where to go next.

The Alphabet
During the first week of school, ride to the dressage letters in alphabetical order. Or make up words using the letters and "ride the words."

Snowman in the Summer
On a really hot summer day, ride three different sized circles in the shape of a snowman and talk about snow.

The Great No Reins Rodeo (very popular!)
This is one of my favorite "new" games. It requires a month or so of practice of steering with the whole body. See Centered Riding materials. I have the riders ride with "ties with eyes", "googly" eyes put on an old necktie to help them remember to use their whole bodies. Eventually they can weave cones with no reins, although the volunteer is always close by. To celebrate no reins riding, we had the No Reins Rodeo consisting of pole bending, barrel racing, and calf roping.

Pole bending: Set up 5 posts in a row. Each rider weaves the posts on the way out, turns around the last post and trots straight back. The rider has hands on hips for weaving, and picks up the reins for trotting back. The volunteer is always near, or has a loose lead.

Barrel racing: The instructor walks the barrel racing pattern. The rider walks around all barrels with hands on hips, then after the third barrel, the rider picks up the reins and trots straight back.

Calf roping: Make a calf with a plastic steer head put on the front of a saw horse. Bailing twine makes a nice tail. Make 8" to 12" diameter circles of rope. The rider walks by the calf and has to toss the rope onto the steer's horns while his horse is walking. No reins, volunteer near or on loose lead.

Get everyone to wear cowboy boots and hats, put Gene Autry on the boom box, and have fun.

Acknowledgements

Thank you to my riders, who put up with the experiments and silliness, crazy hats and weird information.

Thank you to my volunteers, who played along with smiles and made it all possible. Without volunteers there is no therapeutic riding.

Thank you to our selfless equine friends who wore the bunny ears and Santa hats, wove the hula hoops, snagged the pancakes, and ducked the bubbles.

Thank you to Riding to the Top Therapeutic Riding Center in Windham, Maine, for giving me a place to make all this happen.

Thank you to Woody for being my first editor, and to David for wielding the ultimate red pen.

Thank you to Andy for being the best illustrator!

Printed in Great Britain
by Amazon.co.uk, Ltd.,
Marston Gate.